Creating 6-Trait Revisers and Editors for Grade 3

Creating 6-Trait Revisers and Editors for Grade 3

30 Revision and Editing Lessons

Vicki Spandel

Writer in Residence, Great Source Education Group

PEARSON

Boston   New York   San Francisco
Mexico City   Montreal   Toronto   London   Madrid   Munich   Paris
Hong Kong   Singapore   Tokyo   Cape Town   Sydney

Thank you to the following individuals for reviewing this book.

Katie Bell, Central Elementary School
Judy Mazur, Buena Vista Elementary School
Debora Monroe, Bluffsview Elementary School

Executive Editor: Aurora Martínez Ramos
Editorial Assistant: Kara Kikel
Executive Marketing Manager: Krista Clark
Marketing Manager: Danae April
Production Editor: Janet Domingo
Editorial-Production Service: Kathy Smith
Composition Buyer: Linda Cox
Manufacturing Buyer: Megan Cochran
Interior Design and Composition: Schneck-DePippo Graphics
Cover Administrator: Linda Knowles

For related titles and support materials, visit our online catalog at www.allynbaconmerrill.com.

Between the time website information is gathered and then published, it is not unusual for some sites to have closed. Also, the transcription of URLs can result in typographical errors. The publisher would appreciate notification where these errors occur so that they may be corrected in subsequent editions.

ISBN-13: 978-0-205-57059-1   ISBN-10: 0-205-57059-3

Printed in the United States of America
10 9 8 7 6 5 4 3 2 1 Bind-Rite 12 11 10 09 08

**Allyn & Bacon
is an imprint of**

www.allynbaconmerrill.com

Contents

Creating Revisers and Editors

Welcome!

. . . to a series of revision and editing lessons that challenge students to be daring and confident revisers.

These lessons complement and extend instructional ideas found in my books *Creating Writers* (for grades 3 through college) and *Creating Young Writers* (for grades K through 3). Just as I suggest in those books, in these lessons, students practice revision and editing skills on text that is *not their own*, and then extend what they have learned by applying those same strategies to their own writing.

Unlike other writing and revising lessons, this set of lessons shows revision *in action*. It allows students to see drafts in process, observe exactly what a thoughtful reviser does, and compare these revisions to their own revisions of the very same texts. Students work in groups, individually, and with partners, and have multiple chances to experience success.

> Please note that these lessons are a perfect complement to your own instruction or any materials, such as the *Write Traits Classroom Kits* (by Vicki Spandel and Jeff Hicks), that you may use to teach *ideas, organization, voice, word choice, sentence fluency,* and *conventions*.

Why do we need to teach revision differently?

Traditionally, we have not really *taught* revision at all. We have only *assigned* it: "Revise this for Monday." Students who have no idea what to do wind up fixing the conventions (grammar, spelling, and punctuation). This is not revising. It's light editing—at *best*.

The six traits make it possible for us to actually *teach* revision. In order to do so effectively however, we have to make revision visible. This starts with providing rubrics and checklists that clarify expectations. But this is not enough. We must show students what revision looks like, by taking a rough draft and marking it up with arrows, carets, delete symbols, and new text. To understand what makes these lessons different from others, consider what students themselves have said about revision:

"I don't get enough practice!" In most classrooms, students revise *their own work* almost exclusively (though they may offer suggestions to partners). Unless you are a professional writer and you write *every single day* of your life, it is virtually impossible to personally generate enough text to provide the practice needed to become skilled.

"I don't know what people DO when they revise." Many teachers are uncomfortable writing with or in front of students, or are unsure what modeling looks like, and so do not attempt it. As a result, most students have never seen what other writers actually *do* when they revise. Even a thing as simple as double or triple spacing a rough draft (to allow room for revision) may be new to them.

"It feels WAY too big!" Experienced writers revise many things at once, and your students will do this too, eventually. But for beginning writers, being asked to address every issue in a given piece of writing makes revision feel overwhelming. Rather than tackle it, many do nothing at all.

The following lessons address students' needs and anxieties by:

- Allowing them to practice on text that is not their own.
- Showing what revision actually looks like.
- Keeping revision small and manageable.

What if I have never worked with the traits before?

Even if you do not use trait-based instructional materials, you will find this revision and editing practice very student and teacher friendly. If you are not *at all* familiar with the six traits of writing, I urge you to read *Creating Young Writers*, second edition (2008, Pearson Education) or *Creating Writers*, fifth edition (2009, Pearson Education) prior to using these lessons. Remember that the lessons are an extension of these texts. Each text offers numerous student writing samples, descriptions, and additional lesson ideas that will help you understand:

- What the six traits are.
- How they look in primary writing.
- How to use trait language in coaching your student writers.

To get you started, here is a brief description of each trait:

Trait 1

Ideas

Ideas are the heart of the message: the writer's main point or storyline, together with all the details that help make it clear and vivid for the reader.

Trait 2

Organization

Organization is the overall design or structure of the writing, including the lead (or beginning), the flow of ideas, the transitions connecting those ideas, and the conclusion (ending).

Trait 3

Voice

Voice is the writer's unique way of expressing ideas—the general sound and tone of the piece, the link between writer and reader, the verbal fingerprints of the writer on paper.

Trait 4

Word Choice

Word choice includes all the individual words, phrases, and expressions a writer uses to convey ideas and feelings.

Trait 5

Sentence Fluency

Sentence fluency is the flow and rhythm of language, variety in sentences, a natural sound, and the degree to which text can be read with expression and voice.

Trait 6

Conventions

Conventions involve anything a copy editor would take care of to make text easier to process, including (but not limited to) spelling, punctuation, grammar and usage, capitalization, paragraphing, spacing, and layout.

How are the lessons organized?

In this collection, you will find 30 lessons in all, 15 revision lessons and 15 editing lessons. They are alternated so that students practice revision, then editing, then revision again, and so on. Revision lessons are based on the traits of ideas, organization, voice, word choice, and sentence fluency. Editing lessons are based on the trait of conventions.

Each revision lesson is designed to be completed within roughly 40 to 45 minutes. Revision lessons emphasize:

- Sharing of literature.
- Modeling by the teacher.
- Working in pairs.
- Discussion and sharing.

All are designed for use with third grade writers and revisers. If you find a lesson is difficult for some students, you can adjust the amount of revising they do (e.g., add detail in just *one sentence* rather than throughout a paragraph). You can also break a revision lesson into two parts (or even more). For example, you may wish to do the introduction and group revision one day, followed by revision with partners the next day.

Editing lessons are a bit shorter, running about 25 minutes.

In all cases, the intent is that students move from the lesson to working on their own writing, applying the same revision or editing skills.

Lesson Format and Timelines

Each revision lesson contains the following basic components:

- Introduction
- Quotation or sample from literature
- Models A and B for discussion (one strong, one problematic)
- A suggested revision of the weaker model
- A sample for Whole Class Revision (Sample C)
- A suggested revision of Sample C (for you to use in modeling)
- A sample for Revising with Partners (Sample D)
- A suggested revision of Sample D

Preparing for the Lesson. To prepare, read through the entire lesson. Make any copies or overhead transparencies you need. (Note that the general steps and format are the same for each revision lesson and each editing lesson in the set. Once you are familiar with this format, the lesson flow is very easy—and of course, you should personalize each lesson in any way you wish.)

Introducing the Lesson. Each revision lesson begins with (1) a short introduction describing the focus of the lesson, and (2) a brief sample from literature or professional writing to help you illustrate an important writing feature: e.g., *lively verbs.* (If you have access to the literature from which the sample is taken, you may wish to have it handy so you can share additional examples if you so desire.)

Teaching the Lesson. After introducing the lesson, remind students that you will focus on *one kind* of revision strategy. Then follow these steps:

- Share Samples A and B.
- Discuss strengths and problems, determining which is stronger and what students might do to revise the weaker sample (6 minutes).
- *Optional:* Share our suggested revision of the *weaker sample* (3 minutes).
- Share Sample C (*Whole Class Revision*).
- Read Sample C aloud as students follow along OR ask a student to read it aloud (1 minute).
- Invite students to work with partners to identify problems with Sample C, and to make notes they can use to coach you as you model revision of this sample (5 minutes).
- Invite students (as a class) to coach you as you model revision of Sample C (6 minutes). Read your revision aloud to close this portion of the lesson.

> ### Day 1 ends here, if you split the lesson.

- Compare your whole-class revision of Sample C with the suggested revision in the Teacher Notebook (3 minutes).
- Share Sample D (*Revising with Partners*).
- Ask students to revise Sample D independently, following the same strategies they used as a group for Sample C. Then, ask them to check with partners to compare strategies and results (10 minutes).
- Ask two or three pairs of students to share their revisions. The goal is to *hear some variations*, despite use of parallel strategies. (3–4 minutes)
- *Optional:* Compare your revisions to our suggested revision of Sample D. (3 minutes)

Each editing lesson contains the following basic components:

- Introduction and explanation of the focus skill for that lesson
- One or more illustrations you can share with students
- Instructions to guide you step by step through the lesson
- A sample containing actual errors or another conventional problem (e.g., overuse of exclamation points)
- An edited copy that you can compare with your finished editing

Timeline for Editing Lessons. Following is a brief estimate of how long each component of the lesson is likely to take. As with revision lessons, this timeline will vary slightly from class to class:

- Introduce the focus for the lesson (3 minutes).
- Share illustrations (5 minutes).
- Share the Editing Practice sample with students.
- Ask students to edit individually (3–4 minutes).
- Invite students to compare their editing with that of partners (3–4 minutes).
- Invite students (as a class) to coach you as you model editing of the text (3–4 minutes). Read your edited copy aloud.
- Check your editing against our suggested revision (3 minutes).

What if our changes do not agree with the suggested text?

In most cases, your editing should agree *very* closely with our edited copy. In most cases, the edited copy reflects correction of actual errors, such as misuse of apostrophes or incorrect spelling (though some changes, such as replacing an exclamation point with a period, are stylistic). My suggestion is to use a handbook as your final authority, and in the case of any disagreement, consult that handbook. Recommended: *The New Generation Write Source Handbook,* 2006. Wilmington, MA: Great Source Education.

With revision lessons, of course, there are no "correct" answers. What matters is that you and your students identify problems in the text and revise them in a way that makes the draft more clear and readable. The suggested revisions are provided *to guide you*, to make you aware of possibilities, and also to make you more comfortable discussing samples or modeling revision. They are not meant to restrict what you can or should do as writers and revisers.

How do these lessons fit into a writing workshop?

Because they are designed to help students become independent editors and revisers, with a strong grasp of writers' vocabulary, these lessons fit very well into any writing workshop that encourages students to take charge of their own writing process. They are *not* meant to take the place of students' independent writing. Rather, they are intended to serve as a stepping stone into that writing—and to strengthen it.

What can I do to make these lessons more effective?

- **Read *Creating Young Writers*, second edition** (2008, grades K through 3) **or** *Creating Writers,* **fifth edition** (2009, grades 3 through college), and keep a copy handy to refer to as you use these lessons.

- **Keep portfolios/writing folders.**

- **When students have written a draft, let them "abandon" it mentally for a time** by putting it into the writing folder, and doing nothing more with it for three or more days. During this time, present one or more revision/editing lessons. When students return to their drafts, they will see their writing with fresh eyes, and will have in their minds specific skills to apply as they revise. The difference will impress you.

- **Ask students to double or even triple space their own rough drafts,** and to leave large side margins, providing plenty of room for revision or notes. Even if they work on computers, ask them to format drafts in this way. That way, they can make notes on printed copy to guide the revision they will later do electronically.

- **Keep revision small and focused** for third graders. Changing one sentence or inserting one or two details is often enough—unless the student wishes to do more. Do not require re-copying. Think of revision as "playing with the writing." Keep the tone light. Encourage experimentation. Do not expect students to do as much revision as you will see in the examples. Those are provided for discussion purposes to help you and your students see various possibilities. There is *no expectation* that any one student will make every possible revision.

- **Don't plan to revise or assess *everything* students create.** It will be overwhelming for both them and you. Give them lots of writing time, use the lessons to "play" with revision, and allow them to choose an occasional draft of their own to revise. (They will learn and apply many strategies even without prompting from you.)

- **Adapt lessons for challenged writers.** Because the lessons focus on one small aspect of revision, they are already fairly manageable in scope. But you can make them simpler still by (1) asking students who are having difficulty to make only *one* small change, rather than focusing on a full paragraph; (2) ensuring that any student who is struggling has a partner with whom to work, even during those times when other students may be working independently; (3) encouraging struggling students to talk through their ideas for revision before putting anything on paper; and (4) using the recommended literature to provide models (sentences, words, phrases, images, details) that students can refer to or even copy verbatim.

- **Challenge those writers who need it.** Every lesson concludes with a section called "Next Steps," which includes suggestions for challenging those students who are ready for something more difficult.

- **Seat students in a way that makes working in pairs easy and comfortable.**

- **Write with your students,** modeling the kinds of things you would like them to do, such as double spacing copy, changing an ending, or inserting a word or phrase you like better than your original.

- **Provide any auxiliary materials** students might find useful: dictionaries, handbooks, special pens or pencils (erasable) for editing and revision, and so on.

- **Provide additional examples from the literature** you share with your students. One brief example is provided in each lesson, but if you can provide more, you make the use of literary mentors even more powerful.

- **Make yourself as comfortable as possible with the modeling process.** You will have a suggested revision to review in advance, and you can use that suggestion to guide students' responses. However, you should also feel free to be inventive, and to encourage creativity in your students. Your final draft need not look like ours. What matters is for them to see the revision unfold.

- **Help students understand that the revision they do within these lessons is a beginning.** The author of a book might revise a manuscript fifteen times—or more. But the purpose of these lessons is not to create publishable drafts. The purpose is to practice *revision and editing strategies*. On their own, your students will eventually go further than the lessons suggest.

- *Optional:* Once you finish the series of revision lessons, provide students with copies of the 6-Trait Writing Guide for Grade 3. Also provide copies of the Checklist appropriate for the trait you are working on at any given time. Students can use the Writing Guide and/or Checklist as a guide in assessing any writing (including their own) *prior to revision.*

Have fun watching your students' revision and editing skills grow!

Checklists
Creating Revisers and Editors, Grade 3

Note to the Teacher

Following is a series of checklists intended for use with this set of lessons. Use the checklists *one at a time*, as you are teaching the lessons for a particular trait. For example, as you work on the lessons for the trait of ideas, share the Ideas Checklist with students and encourage them to use it when revising their own work. After you teach the lessons for another trait, share the checklist for *that trait*. In this way, you gradually add new revision possibilities.

Encourage honesty! Good writers make *numerous changes* to their text. So in filling out a checklist, the object is not to be perfect, but to be such a good reader of your own work that you know how to tackle revision. It helps if you model this with a piece of your own writing.

Keep it manageable. Once students have more than one checklist going, it is a good idea to think about how many things they should take on at once. Working on too much at once tends to distract or overwhelm many young writers. Addressing one or two problems thoroughly, on the other hand, can improve a draft measurably.

How is a checklist different from a writing guide? This set of lessons also includes a Writing Guide designed specially for third grade. You are welcome to use it—or not. Some third grade teachers prefer checklists because they have no numbers on them. They are simply reminders of which features are important in relation to each trait. The Writing Guide includes those same features along a six-point continuum, on which a score of 1 signifies *not failure*, but a beginning effort—something on paper for which a point is awarded. Scores of 1, 2, or 3 indicate fairly significant need for revision. Scores of 4, 5, or 6 indicate strength with respect to the trait at hand.

It is not necessary for you to use this Writing Guide unless you feel it is appropriate for your students and you think they will find it fun and helpful to work with. If you do decide to use it, ask them to (1) score the writing of anonymous writers (such as those whose work appears in these lessons), or (2) score their own writing *in preparation for revision—not* for grading purposes. Do *not* ask them to score each other's writing. This can create confusion—and sometimes hurt feelings as well. Assessment for grading purposes should remain your responsibility.

A Writing Guide is just that: a guide to help you see how strong your own work is along a continuum of performance, and to help you understand the kinds of problems writers face when they revise. Remember, the purpose of these lessons is to create revisers, not critics. The discussion that comes out of assessing a piece of work and talking about it with others, however, is extremely helpful in giving writers the insight they need to improve their work.

Organization

—— Strong lead—makes you want to read more

—— Strong ending—makes you think

—— Order that is easy to follow

Ideas

—— Clear—makes sense

—— Helpful details you'll remember

—— Details of sound, sight, smell, touch, taste

—— Focus on ONE main topic or story

Personal Revision Guide

Word Choice

—— **Words that are "just right"**

—— **Lively verbs**

—— **Pictures and movies in the reader's mind**

Personal Revision Guide

Voice

—— **Expressive**

—— **Sounds like ME**

—— **Confident**

—— **Speaks to readers**

Please note . . .
No checklist is included for Conventions because it appears in conjunction with the editing lessons.

Personal Revision Guide

Sentence Fluency

—— Sentences begin in different ways

—— Some long, some short

—— No repetition—no unneeded words

Student Writing Guide, Grade 3

Ideas

6
- ☐ Every line of my writing makes sense.
- ☐ I stick to one topic or story.
- ☐ I chose my details carefully. They will get your attention.

5
- ☐ My main message is clear.
- ☐ I stick to one topic or story.
- ☐ I share a lot of details.

4
- ☐ My writing is clear more often than not.
- ☐ I *mostly* wrote about one topic or story.
- ☐ I came up with a few good details.

3
- ☐ Some parts of my writing could be more clear.
- ☐ I had a *little trouble* sticking to my main topic.
- ☐ It was hard to come up with enough details.

2
- ☐ This writing is confusing.
- ☐ I kept going off the topic.
- ☐ I guessed about details—sometimes I made things up.

1
- ☐ It's hard to tell what I am talking about.
- ☐ I am not sure what my topic is.
- ☐ I wrote whatever came into my head.

Organization

6
- ☐ My lead makes you want to keep reading.
- ☐ My ending will leave you thinking.
- ☐ Every single detail comes in the right order.

5
- ☐ My lead is good.
- ☐ My ending is strong, too.
- ☐ My writing is easy to follow.

4
- ☐ I have a lead. It works.
- ☐ My ending is fine, too.
- ☐ You can follow this if you read carefully.

3
- ☐ My lead could be more exciting.
- ☐ My ending needs work.
- ☐ Some things seem out of order.

2
- ☐ My lead is one everybody uses: *This is a paper about* . . .
- ☐ My ending repeats things I already said.
- ☐ This *is very hard* to follow. The order is not working.

1
- ☐ I don't have a lead. It just starts.
- ☐ I don't have an ending. It just stops.
- ☐ I put things in *any* old order. I don't know what the best order is!

Student Writing Guide, Grade 3

Voice

6
- ☐ This is lively and expressive. It sounds just like ME.
- ☐ I sound very confident. I know my topic. I mean what I say.
- ☐ I know just who my readers are—the voice is right for them.

5
- ☐ This has expressive parts. I think it sounds like me.
- ☐ I sound confident. I know my topic fairly well.
- ☐ I tried to make the voice fit my readers.

4
- ☐ You can tell I wrote this. I hear my voice often.
- ☐ Parts of my paper sound confident.
- ☐ You can tell I'm thinking of the reader most of the time.

3
- ☐ I hear my own voice once or twice.
- ☐ I wish I knew this topic better—then I'd sound confident.
- ☐ I wasn't *always* thinking of the reader. I just wrote.

2
- ☐ My voice is quiet. I'm not writing like "I mean it."
- ☐ I need a LOT more information to sound confident.
- ☐ This might not be the right voice for my readers.

1
- ☐ This doesn't sound like me at all. This could be *anybody*!
- ☐ I do not sound confident—because I don't know this topic.
- ☐ I don't know who my readers are. I can't picture them.

Word Choice

6
- ☐ I stretched for *just* the right words. You'll remember them!
- ☐ I used a LOT of lively verbs.
- ☐ My words make pictures and movies in your mind.

5
- ☐ I chose interesting words. They make my message clear.
- ☐ I have many lively verbs.
- ☐ My words will help you picture things.

4
- ☐ My writing is clear. I used words correctly.
- ☐ I have *some* lively verbs. You'll get the main idea.
- ☐ I created at least one good "snapshot."

3
- ☐ Most of my words are correct. They might not be the *best* words.
- ☐ The verbs could be stronger.
- ☐ You'll need some imagination to picture things.

2
- ☐ I used words everyone uses: *nice, good, special, fun.*
- ☐ I need more verbs. Everything is *is, are, was, were.*
- ☐ You'll need to make up your own pictures!

1
- ☐ I wasn't sure what words to use. What's my message?
- ☐ I'm not sure if I have verbs or not.
- ☐ I don't have a clear picture in *my own mind* yet.

Student Writing Guide, Grade 3

Sentence Fluency

6
- ☐ Almost every sentence starts in a different way.
- ☐ I have a good mix of long and short sentences.
- ☐ Every word counts. I wouldn't cut *anything*.

5
- ☐ Many of my sentences begin in different ways.
- ☐ I have some long sentences and some shorter sentences.
- ☐ My writing is not wordy.

4
- ☐ Some sentences begin in different ways.
- ☐ A few sentences are longer than others.
- ☐ I have some repetition. I could cut a few words.

3
- ☐ A LOT of my sentences begin the same way.
- ☐ My sentences are mostly long—or mostly short!
- ☐ I repeated things—or used more words than I needed.

2
- ☐ *Most* of my sentences begin the same way.
- ☐ They're ALL long—or they're ALL short.
- ☐ I used way too many words—or else I didn't write enough!

1
- ☐ I could only think of one way to start my sentences. OR,
- ☐ I just wrote one BIG sentence. OR,
- ☐ I can't tell where the sentences start or stop.

Conventions

6
- ☐ I edited this thoroughly. I read it silently and aloud.
- ☐ You'd have to be very picky to find errors!
- ☐ This is **ready to publish.**

5
- ☐ I edited this. I read it aloud.
- ☐ If I have errors, they are small and hard to spot.
- ☐ This only needs a **light touchup.**

4
- ☐ I read through my paper and fixed a few things.
- ☐ It still has *some* errors, but they don't block my message.
- ☐ I need to **go over it again** before it's published.

3
- ☐ I skimmed my paper. I did not read it aloud.
- ☐ I fixed a few errors I noticed.
- ☐ This piece needs **careful editing** before it's published.

2
- ☐ I barely looked at my paper.
- ☐ I think it still has many errors.
- ☐ I need to **read it aloud and use a ruler** to help me find errors.

1
- ☐ After I finished writing, I did not look at my paper again.
- ☐ I need help editing. I don't know how many errors I have.
- ☐ I need to **work with a partner** to help me find errors.

Bibliography

List of Books Referenced for Grade 3 Lesson Set

Baylor, Byrd. 1995. *I'm in Charge of Celebrations.* New York: Aladdin.

Baylor, Byrd. 1985. *Everybody Needs a Rock.* New York: Aladdin.

Baylor, Byrd. 1998. *The Table Where the Rich People Sit.* New York: Aladdin.

Blume, Judy. 1971. *Freckle Juice.* New York: Random House.

Cannon, Janell. 2000. *Crickwing.* New York: Harcourt.

Cannon, Janell. 1997. *Verdi.* New York: Harcourt.

Child, Lauren. 2004. *Clarice Bean Spells Trouble.* Cambridge, MA: Candlewick Press.

Collard, Sneed B. III. 2000. *A Whale Biologist at Work.* New York: Franklin Watts.

Collard, Sneed B. III. 1997. *Creepy Creatures.* Watertown, MA: Charlesbridge.

Cronin, Doreen. 2000. *Click, Clack, Moo: Cows That Type.* New York: Simon & Schuster.

Cronin, Doreen. 2005. *Diary of a Spider.* New York: HarperCollins.

Dahl, Roald. 1998. *Matilda.* New York: Puffin.

Dahl, Roald. 2007 (reprint edition). *The Twits.* New York: Puffin.

DiCamillo, Kate. 2000. *Because of Winn-Dixie.* Cambridge, MA: Candlewick Press.

DiCamillo, Kate. 2003. *The Tale of Despereaux.* Cambridge, MA: Candlewick Press.

Drachman, Eric. 2005. *A Frog Thing.* Los Angeles: Kidwick Books.

Fletcher, Ralph. 1997. *Twilight Comes Twice.* Boston: Clarion Books.

Florian, Douglas. 1996. *On the Wing: Bird Poems and Paintings.* Orlando: Harcourt.

George, Jean Craighead. 1992. *The Missing 'Gator of Gumbo Limbo.* New York: HarperCollins.

George, Twig. 2001. *Jellies.* Minneapolis: Millbrook Press.

George, Twig. 2003. *Seahorses.* Minneapolis: Millbrook Press.

Grimes, Nikki. 1999. *My Man Blue.* New York: Dial Books for Young Readers.

Hamanaka, Sheila. 1999. *All the Colors of the Earth.* New York: HarperTrophy.

Harness, Cheryl. 2005. *The Remarkable Benjamin Franklin.* Washington, D.C.: National Geographic.

Jenkins, Alvin. 2004. *Next Stop Neptune.* Boston: Houghton Mifflin.

Kniedel, Sally Stenhouse. 1993. *Creepy Crawlies and the Scientific Method.* New York: Fulcrum Publishing.

Kramer, Stephen. 1992. *Tornado.* Minneapolis: Carolrhoda Books.

Marcellino, Fred. 2002. *I, Crocodile.* New York: HarperTrophy.

Markle, Sandra. 2006. *A Mother's Journey.* Watertown, MA: Charlesbridge.

Marshall, James. 2000. *George and Martha.* Boston: Houghton Mifflin.

Nye, Bill. 2003. *Bill Nye the Science Guy's Big Blue Ocean.* New York: Hyperion.

Nye, Bill. 2002. *Bill Nye the Science Guy's Great Big Dinosaur Dig.* New York: Hyperion.

Nye, Bill. 2005. Bill Nye the Science Guy's Great Big Book of Tiny Germs. New York: Hyperion.

Nye, Bill. 1993. Bill Nye the Science Guy's Big Blast of Science. Mercer Island, WA: TVbooks, Inc.

O'Malley, Kevin. 2005. Once Upon a Cool Motorcycle Dude. New York: Walker and Company.

Paulsen, Gary. 1995. Dogteam. New York: Delacorte Press.

Pitcher, Caroline. 2004. Lord of the Forest. London: Frances Lincoln Children's Books.

Rylant, Cynthia. 1991. Night in the Country. New York: Aladdin.

Schotter, Roni. 1997. Nothing Ever Happens on 90th Street. New York: Scholastic.

Simon, Seymour. 2000. Bones: Our Skeletal System. New York: Harper Trophy.

Simon, Seymour. 2006. The Heart: Our Circulatory System. New York: HarperCollins.

Simon, Seymour. 2006. Our Solar System. New York: HarperCollins.

Simon, Seymour. 2006. Whales. New York: HarperCollins.

Steig, William. 1992. Amos and Boris. New York: Farrar, Straus & Giroux.

Steig, William. 1982. Dr. DeSoto. New York: Farrar, Straus & Giroux.

Stevens, Janet. 2005. The Great Fuzz Frenzy. New York: Harcourt.

Teague, Mark. 2002. Dear Mrs LaRue: Letters from Obedience School. New York: Scholastic.

Viorst, Judith. 1981. If I Were in Charge of the World and other worries. New York: Simon & Schuster.

Wesley, Valerie Wilson. 2004. How to Fish for Trouble (Willemena Rules!). New York: Hyperion.

Weston, Carol. 2001. The Diary of Melanie Martin: Or How I Survived Matt the Brat, Michelangelo and the Leaning Tower of Pizza. New York: Yearling.

White, E. B. 1952 (renewed 1980). Charlotte's Web. New York: HarperCollins.

Yolen, Jane. 1997. Sleeping Ugly. New York: Putnam.

Lessons for Grade 3

*Indicates editing lesson.

Using the Caret ∧

Trait Connection: **Conventions**

Introduction (Share with students in your own words)

The caret looks like a small arrow (∧). It is one of the handiest symbols an editor can use. It shows that a letter, word, phrase, or sentence should be inserted into a document. The caret helps a writer who forgets something or wants to make a change. Here is an example:

Bob saw a big running down street.

Two words are missing from this sentence. This is easy to fix, using carets:

dog   *the*
Bob saw a big∧running down∧street.

If you are editing right on a computer, you won't use the caret, of course; it is only used with printed text. Nevertheless, practice using the caret trains you to think and read like an editor. It will help you spot those little missing words!

Teaching the Lesson (General Guidelines for Teachers)

1. Show students what the caret (∧) looks like.

2. Practice writing a caret and using it to insert a word, letter, or sentence. (Use our sample sentence above, or make up your own.)

3. Share the editing lesson on the following page. Notice that the ONLY errors in this lesson are those *calling for insertions*. Students will insert missing letters or words. They do not need to make *any other changes*.

4. Ask them to work individually first, then check with a partner.

5. When everyone is done, ask them to coach you as you edit the copy on a whiteboard or overhead transparency.

6. When you finish, check your editing against the corrected copy on page 22.

Editing Goals:
Catch 5 (or more) of 8 errors.
Look for missing words or letters in your own writing.

Editing Practice

Lesson 1: Using the caret (^)
Missing words or letters

Joe and Bill playing soccer. The were having

a great time. Bill kicked a field goal. Th ball

went flying into net. "Wow!" yelled Joe. "That

was a terrific kick!" The ball had gone right

over dog that was running across field.

Bill could not believe he had kicked the ball

that hard. "I think that was my best goal ever," he.

They home for pizza.

Corrected Copy

Lesson 1: Using the Caret
8 errors

Joe and Bill ^were^ playing soccer. The^y^ were having

a great time. Bill kicked a field goal. Th^e^ ball

went flying into ^the^ net. "Wow!" yelled Joe. "That

was a terrific kick!" The ball had gone right

over ^a^ dog that was running across ^the^ field.

Bill could not believe he had kicked the ball

that hard. "I think that was my best goal ever," he^said^.

They ^went^ home for pizza.

Revising for Detail

Trait Connection: **Ideas**

Introduction

Writing without details is like a blank piece of paper—all white space with nothing to look at. Readers like writers to answer their questions—to fill in the "white space." Suppose we start with a tree. Can you picture it yet? The trunk is jet black and thick as a barrel. It's an oak, 25 feet high with wide, spreading branches like giant arms and light green leaves. Halfway up, if you peek through the leaves, you'll see a robin's nest holding three blue speckled eggs. Now we're getting somewhere. In this lesson, you will revise by filling the white space, adding the kinds of details that make writing interesting.

Teacher's Sidebar . . .

The *number* of details is not as important as the *quality* of those details. Good writers do not try to pack in as many details as possible, but rather choose one or two (or possibly more) details that *make a difference*.

Focus and Intent

This lesson is intended to help students:

- Understand the concept of "detail."
- Recognize detail in the writing of others.
- Develop skills in revising by adding or enriching detail.

Teaching the Lesson

Step 1: Introducing the Concept of Detail

What *is* a detail anyway? Ask students to help you define the concept of "detail" by listing all the different kinds of *little information* writers share with us. Your list might include any or all of the following (feel free to add your own ideas to these):

- sounds
- feelings
- smells
- tastes
- textures

- colors
- shapes
- other facts

Step 2: Making the Reading-Writing Connection

Share the following example from literature, or share a favorite passage of your own. Ask students to identify what they *see, hear, smell,* or *feel*. If they have been to a fair, ask what other details the author might have included. For instance, what things might you *feel* at a fair?

Example

When they pulled into the Fair Grounds, they could hear music and see the Ferris Wheel turning in the sky. They could smell the dust of the race track where the sprinkling cart had moistened it; and they could smell hamburgers frying and see balloons aloft. They could hear sheep blatting in their pens.

(E. B. White, *Charlotte's Web*. 1952. Renewed 1980. New York: HarperCollins Publishers, page 130.)

Step 3: Involving Students as Evaluators

Ask students to review Samples A and B, specifically looking for vivid details: what's easy to picture, what's interesting. Have students work with a partner, highlighting details in each example that stand out. Encourage them to write any unanswered questions in the margin.

Discussing Results

Most students should find Sample B significantly stronger. Discuss differences between A and B, asking students to share any passages they highlighted from either sample. Ask what details they liked especially well in Sample B, and what questions were not answered in Sample A.

Step 4: Modeling Revision

- Share Sample C (*Whole Class Revision*) with students. Read it aloud.
- Remind students that good writers need to *think like readers,* asking, "Does this writing answer a reader's questions? Does it fill in the white space?"
- With students' help, identify one or two samples of *details that work*. Then, with their coaching, underline two or three short passages that need sharper details.
- Ask students for suggestions, and write them into the draft copy. Use cross-outs and/or carets (^) and arrows to create your revision so students see how to mark up copy.
- When you finish, read your revised passage aloud. (You may compare your revised version with our suggestion, keeping in mind that ours is *only a suggestion*.)

Step 5: Revising with Partners

Share Sample D (*Revising with Partners*). Ask students to work with partners, following the basic steps you modeled with Sample C. *Working with partners,* they should:

- Highlight what is working now.
- Underline passages that need stronger detail.
- Revise by crossing out any vague words and inserting new details.

Step 6: Sharing and Discussing Results

When students have finished, ask several pairs of students to share their revisions aloud and discuss the kinds of changes they have made. Emphasize the vividness of revised details, or students' ability to come up with details others did not think of. This is more important than the *number* of changes made.

Next Steps

- Remind students to *always* create rough drafts with double- or triple-spaced copy and wide margins to make revision easier.

- As soon as possible following this lesson, ask students to revise a piece of their own writing, using this same technique. Remind them that the number of details is not as significant as the quality of those details.

- Listen for samples of quality detail in any literature you share. Recommended:
  - *Charlotte's Web* by E. B. White. 1952 (renewed 1980). New York: HarperCollins.
  - *Night in the Country* by Cynthia Rylant. 1991. New York: Aladdin.
  - *Twilight Comes Twice* by Ralph Fletcher. 1997. Boston: Clarion Books.
  - *The Twits* by Roald Dahl. 2007 (reprint edition). New York: Puffin.

- *For students who need a challenge:* What might it look like when a tiny spider hatches from an egg sac? Even if none of your students have seen this, they can imagine it. Ask them to write an imagined description. Then, compare what they write to E. B. White's description, Chapter XXII, "A Warm Wind," page 177, from *Charlotte's Web*. Ask your students if they think E. B. White actually watched spiders hatch prior to writing this. (Yes, he did.) How does experience help writers put more detail in their writing?

- *For an additional challenge:* Create an experience of your own to use as the basis for writing. You can start with an observation of something in your classroom (a plant, animal, or fish), a visit (from a baby or pet, for example), or the experience of a film or field trip. Experience *first,* taking in the details—*then* write. Watch those details unfold!

Sample A

Joey wasn't too sure about this.

The fence looked hard to climb.

On the other side he could see something.

He heard an interesting sound

coming from somewhere. He

went over the fence.

Sample B

Iris stood on the diving board—backwards. Her toes clung to the rough white mat. Her heels hung out over the edge. It looked like a mile to the pool below. The water was shimmering like a big blue Jell-O. "Dive!" she heard her coach yell. All the kids were watching. She could feel their eyes on her. She closed her own eyes and made a wish. She wished she were at her grandmother's house, baking cookies. "Dive!" she heard again—and then the music faded and she felt the cold air rush along her body.

Suggested Revision of Sample A

Joey wasn't too sure about this.

old board   tall, rough, and rickety.

The fence looked ~~hard to climb.~~

a tiny gray shed.

On the other side he could see ~~something.~~

a soft whining

He heard ~~an interesting~~ sound

inside the shed.   took a deep breath

coming from ~~somewhere.~~ He

and scrambled

~~went~~ over the fence.

Sample C: Whole Class Revision

When Mara brought out the small washtub, Tiger looked upset. He sounded upset, too. His eyes got big. Mara got her arms around Tiger's body. He moved a lot. She got him into the tub. He made a lot of noise.

Sample D: Revision with Partners

Arliss had never changed a baby. What if

something happened? Reuben cried a lot!

It bothered Arliss. She put him on the

changing table. His diaper was very wet.

She got a new one on and pulled the

Velcro tabs. She was so glad everything

went OK.

Suggested Revisions of C and D

Sample C: Whole Class Revision

When Mara brought out the small
flexed his claws and his hair stood on end.
washtub, Tiger ~~looked upset.~~ He
meowed fiercely.   *the size of quarters!*
~~sounded upset, too.~~ His eyes got ~~big.~~

Mara got her arms around Tiger's
squirmed and wriggled, but
body. He ~~moved a lot.~~ She got him
hissed at her through the bubbles.
into the tub. He ~~made a lot of noise.~~

Sample D: Revising with Partners

Arliss had never changed a baby. What if
he fell?   *so hard he turned bright red!*
~~something happened?~~ Reuben cried ~~a lot!~~
made Arliss's ears hurt!
It ~~bothered Arliss.~~ She put him on the
as wet as a sponge!
changing table. His diaper was ~~very wet.~~

She got a new one on and pulled the
snug and tight.
Velcro tabs. She was so glad everything
that she gave Reuben a huge hug.
went OK.

Using the Delete Symbol (6)

Trait Connection: **Conventions**

Introduction (Share with students in your own words)

The delete symbol looks like a line with a small curl at the end (6). Editors use the delete symbol horizontally to take out an extra word, and vertically to take out a repeated letter. Here are two examples:

Fern could not not swimm.

Without meaning to, the writer repeated the word *not* and the letter *m*. These small problems are easy to fix using the delete symbol:

Fern could not <s>not</s> swimm.

Practice using this symbol is helpful because it reminds you, as a writer and editor, to look and listen carefully for repeated words or letters. Don't forget: Read *everything* you write aloud.

Teaching the Lesson (General Guidelines for Teachers)

1. Show students what the delete symbol (6) looks like.

2. Practice writing a delete symbol and using it to take out a word or letter that is repeated. (Use our sample sentence above, or make up your own examples.)

3. Share the editing lesson on the following page. Notice that the ONLY errors in this lesson are those *calling for deletions*. Students will delete repeated letters or words. They do not need to make *any other changes*.

4. Ask them to work individually first, then check with a partner.

5. When everyone is done, ask them to coach you as you edit the copy on an overhead transparency.

6. When you finish, check your editing against the corrected copy on page 34.

Editing Goal: Make 5 or more of 8 needed deletions.
Next, look for repeated words or letters in your own work!

Editing Practice

Using the delete symbol (⸮)
Delete repeated words or letters

Sara and Gus went went fishing. Sara had been

fishing maany times with her Uncle Xavier. But for

Gus, it was was the very first time. They held

long fishing poles made of bamboo. The fishing

poles had lines made of thin cord and and hooks on

on the end. They waited forever, but nothing

happened. Finally, Guss felt a small tug on his line—

then then a bigger tug. "Be extra quiet!" Sara

whispered. "Don't scare the the fish."

Corrected Copy

Using the delete symbol ($\mathscr{e}$)
8 repeated words or letters

Sara and Gus went ~~went~~ fishing. Sara had been

fishing ma~~n~~y times with her Uncle Xavier. But for

Gus, it was ~~was~~ the very first time. They held

long fishing poles made of bamboo. The fishing

poles had lines made of thin cord and ~~and~~ hooks on

~~on~~ the end. They waited forever, but nothing

happened. Finally, Gus~~s~~ felt a small tug on his line—

then ~~then~~ a bigger tug. "Be extra quiet!" Sara

whispered. "Don't scare the ~~the~~ fish."

Revising for Clarity

Trait Connection: **Ideas**

Introduction

When writing is unclear, the reader has to work to figure out what the writer means. Suppose a writer describes an experience skiing downhill as "just wild!" Does this mean it was exciting and thrilling? Or does it mean it was terrifying and the writer felt afraid? Good writing provides *enough information*—and the *right information*—to make the message clear. In this lesson, you will practice revising a vague example so that the reader isn't left wondering what the passage was all about.

> ### Teacher's Sidebar . . .
> When writing is clear, readers never say to themselves, "What does the writer *mean?*" They know. Before revising anything in writing, therefore, it is helpful to discuss, as a class, what the writer is trying to say—and then say the message *out loud*. If you can *say* it clearly, you'll have a much easier time *writing* it clearly.

Focus and Intent

This lesson is intended to help students:

- Understand the concept of "clarity."
- Recognize clarity in a sample of writing.
- Develop skills in revising for clarity.

Teaching the Lesson

Step 1: Introducing the Concept of Clarity

Work with students to define the concept of clarity through a series of examples. Begin with a vague word or expression on the left, and clarify by coming up with a more precise word or expression; list that on the right. One example is provided for you. Think creatively!

- The music <u>was loud</u>.   The music <u>hurt my ears</u>.
- The movie <u>seemed long</u>.   _____
- The pizza <u>was different</u>.   _____
- The weather <u>surprised us</u>.   _____

Step 2: Making the Reading-Writing Connection

Share the following suggested sample from literature, or any favorite passage of your own. Ask students to first state the writer's intended meaning or message (*This tree is huge and very special to the writer*), then to identify any words, details, or examples that help make that meaning clear. What strategies does this writer employ that students could use in their own writing?

Sample

Mom and I live in a yellow wall tent under the most beautiful live oak in Collier County. The oak is so big Mom and I, even by holding hands, cannot reach each other around the tree. Its limbs would cover a tennis court.

(Jean Craighead George, *The Missing 'Gator of Gumbo Limbo.* 1992. New York: HarperCollins Children's Books, pages 9–10.)

Step 3: Involving Students as Evaluators

Ask students to review Samples A and B, specifically looking for clarity: words or phrases, examples, or comparisons that each writer uses to make meaning clear. Have students work with a partner, highlighting passages from each sample that add to clarity. Encourage them to write notes, comments, or questions in the right margin as they read.

Discussing Results

Most students should find Sample A significantly stronger. Discuss differences between A and B, asking students to summarize the meaning of each and to say which is more clear and why. Ask what they liked especially well in Sample A, and what could be revised in Sample B. A suggested revision of Sample B is provided.

Step 4: Modeling Revision

- Share Sample C (*Whole Class Revision*) with students. Read it aloud.
- Ask students whether it is clear. (Most should say *no.*) Remind students to *think like readers* as they coach you through a revision. With their coaching, underline one or two short passages that could be rewritten by using other words or adding an example or comparison to make the meaning clear. Write your revisions into the draft copy.
- When you finish, read your revised passage aloud. (You may compare your revised version with our suggestion, but *make sure they know ours is ONLY a suggestion.*)

Step 5: Revising with Partners

Share Sample D (*Revising with Partners*). Ask students to follow the basic steps you modeled with Sample C. *Working with partners,* they should:

- Read the passage aloud.
- Highlight what is working now.
- Underline one or two (or more) passages that need revision.
- Revise by crossing out any vague words or phrases, and using new words or adding examples or comparisons to enhance clarity.

Step 6: Sharing and Discussing Results

When students have finished, ask several pairs of students to share their revisions aloud and discuss the kinds of changes they have made. (Again, feel free to share our suggested revision if that is helpful.) Emphasize originality of expression or use of examples. Who found a way to make meaning clear that no one else thought of?

Next Steps

- Remind students to routinely create rough drafts with double- or triple-spaced copy and wide margins to make revision easier.

- As soon as possible following this lesson, ask students to revise a piece of their own writing for clarity. Remind them about specific strategies they can use to increase clarity: precise words, examples, comparisons.

- Listen for examples of clarity in any literature you share. Encourage students to point them out. Clarity is of particular importance in informational writing (such as you might find in a textbook or informational journal) or in directions. Recommended:

  - *The Missing 'Gator of Gumbo Limbo* by Jean Craighead George. 1992. New York: HarperCollins.
  - *Creepy Crawlies and the Scientific Method* by Sally Stenhouse Kniedel. 1993. New York: Fulcrum Publishing.
  - *Our Solar System* by Seymour Simon. 2006. New York: Collins.
  - *A Whale Biologist at Work* by Sneed B. Collard III. 2000. New York: Franklin Watts.

- *For students who need a challenge:* Invite students to research any informational question on any topic either online or through your library. Ask them to write from three to six sentences on their topics, going for clarity! Remember: It helps to use precise language, to explain terms the reader might not know (notice the word "pack" in Sample A, defined as a "group"), to give the reader examples, and to make comparisons with things the reader might find familiar.

Sample A

Wolves live in the forests of Canada and Northern Minnesota. They live in packs, or large groups. A pack of wolves can work together to hunt large game like moose. Wolves are social animals that take care of each other's pups. In this way, they are not unlike people, who babysit other people's children. Some people are afraid of wolves, but wolves are actually shy and avoid people.

Sample B

Squirrels are smart animals. They live

in many places. They find food

anywhere they live. They eat many

things. You can tell squirrels are friendly.

Suggested Revision of Sample B

Squirrels are smart animals. They live
almost anywhere from forests to cities.
~~in many places.~~ They find food
                              nuts, berries, and seeds.
anywhere they live. They eat ~~many things.~~
                because they will come right up to you and
You can tell squirrels are friendly. beg for handouts!

Sample C: Whole Class Revision

Mosquitoes move fast. Sometimes many land on a person at once. A human does not always hear a mosquito coming or feel it land. The mosquito injects a numbing substance so the person does not feel the bite. Later, you can see the bite and feel it, too.

Sample D: Revising with Partners

People use computers for many things. Some use them to send e-mails. People also use computers to get information on any subject you can think of. Computers are helpful.

Suggested Revisions of C and D

Sample C: Whole Class Revision

Mosquitoes ~~move fast.~~ (zoom along in swarms.) Sometimes ~~many land on a~~ (hundreds cover a)

person ~~at once.~~ (like a blanket.) A human does not always hear a

mosquito coming or feel it land. The mosquito injects a

numbing substance so the person does not feel the bite.

Later, ~~you can see~~ the bite (turns flaming red and itches like fire!) ~~and feel it, too.~~

Sample D: Revising with Partners

People use computers for ~~many things.~~ (everything from writing to shopping.) Some use

them to send e-mails. People also use computers to

get information on any subject you can think of. (from sports to space.)

Computers ~~are helpful.~~ (help us learn about the world and organize our lives.)

Putting In (^), Taking Out (ↄ)

Lesson 5

Trait Connection: Conventions

Introduction (Share with students in your own words)

Sometimes a writer or editor uses a delete symbol to take out one thing, and a caret to insert something else. These changes are not *always* about correcting errors. Sometimes, the writer simply wants to say something a different way. Here is an example:

The elephant was very big.

Let's say the writer decides that *very big* is not a good way to describe an elephant. She wants something stronger. So she marks the copy this way:

enormous.
The elephant was ^ ~~very big.~~

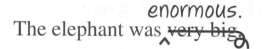

Using the caret and delete symbol together gives writers and editors freedom to say things just the way they want to. That's what revision is all about.

Teaching the Lesson (General Guidelines for Teachers)

1. Remind students what the caret (^) and delete symbol (ↄ) look like.
2. Practice using both in the same sentence. (Use our sample sentence above, or make up your own.)
3. Share the editing lesson on the following page. This lesson contains NO actual errors. Students should read the passage and make their own editorial changes about *anything* they wish to take out or put in.
4. Ask them to work individually first, then check with a partner.
5. When everyone is done, ask them to coach you as you edit the same copy, using the caret and delete symbol.
6. When you finish, compare your edited text to ours on page 46.

Editing Goal: Create copy you like better.
Next, look for changes you'd like to make in your own work.

Revision Practice

Using the caret (^)
Using the delete symbol (✗)

Isabel went to the zoo with her Uncle Ahmed. They saw many animals. Isabel liked the monkeys the best. She thought they were funny. They swung from ropes and made noises at her. She tossed them some food. They liked it! Uncle Ahmed laughed very hard.

Sample Revision

Using the Caret and Delete Symbol Together
No errors—all revisions are optional

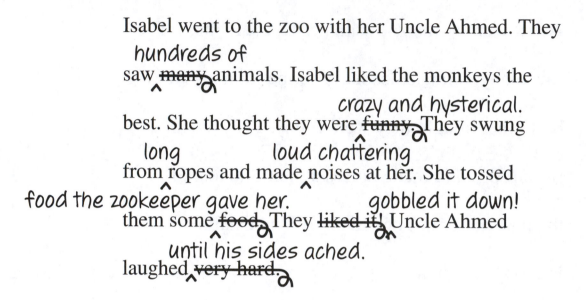

Isabel went to the zoo with her Uncle Ahmed. They
saw ~~many~~ ^hundreds of^ animals. Isabel liked the monkeys the
best. She thought they were ~~funny.~~ ^crazy and hysterical.^ They swung
from ropes and made ^long^ noises ^loud chattering^ at her. She tossed
them some ~~food.~~ ^food the zookeeper gave her.^ They ~~liked it!~~ ^gobbled it down!^ Uncle Ahmed
laughed ^until his sides ached.^ ~~very hard.~~

> **Note**
> Many other revisions are possible. Did you
> think of some we did not? If so, good for you!

Revising for Focus

Trait Connection: **Ideas**

Introduction

Writers sometimes begin to tell one story or make one point—and then wander unexpectedly in another direction. How confusing! In this lesson, you will practice revising to stay focused on *one main topic*.

> Teacher's Sidebar . . .
> It is entirely possible to tell two (or more) *related* stories or make two points that are *closely connected*. Writers get into trouble when they do not show how things connect—or when they switch topics completely and there *is no real connection* to be made.

Focus and Intent

This lesson is intended to help students:

- Understand the concept of "focus."
- Recognize focus or lack of focus in writing.
- Develop skills in revising for focus.

Teaching the Lesson

Step 1: Introducing the Concept of Focus

1. Begin by identifying *any topic* that might be of interest to your student writers. With their help, create a web of potentially related sub-topics a writer might explore within *one* paragraph, essay, or story. For example, let's say your central topic is "dogs." Your web might look something like the example on the following page.

2. Next, working together, make a list of *totally unrelated topics*. Have fun. But remember—sometimes there is a connection you do not see at first. So, for each sub-topic, ask students, "*Could* this be connected to our main idea?" If

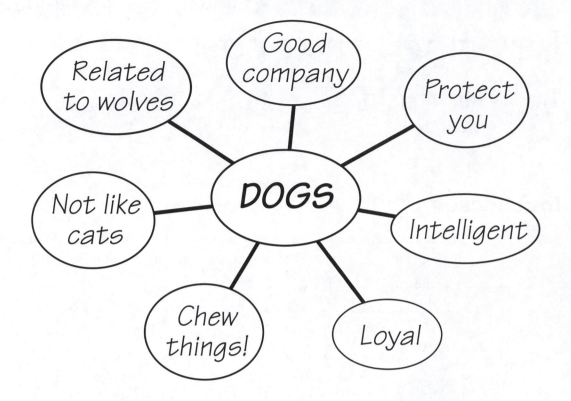

you see a connection after all, add it to the web. If you do not see *any connection*, put it on the "Save for another time" list. If your topic is "dogs," your "Save for another time" list might look like this:

Save for another time . . .

- My favorite relative
- Field trip to the cheese factory
- How to care for goldfish
- Volcanoes

Step 2: Making the Reading-Writing Connection

Share the following suggested sample from literature, or any favorite passage of your own. Ask students to identify the focus of the passage (*Winn-Dixie needs a bath but doesn't like it*) and then to say whether, in their opinion, the author stays true to this focus.

Sample

I started in on Winn-Dixie right away, trying to clean him up. First, I gave him a bath. I used the garden hose and some baby shampoo. He stood still for it, but I could tell he didn't like it. He looked insulted, and the whole time he didn't show me his teeth or wag his tail once.

(Kate DiCamillo, *Because of Winn-Dixie*. 2000. Cambridge, MA: Candlewick Press, page 20.)

Step 3: Involving Students as Evaluators

Ask students to review Samples A and B, specifically checking for focus. Have students work with a partner, highlighting any passage from either sample that seems to wander off-track. Encourage them to make notes—comments or questions—in the right margin as they read.

Discussing Results

Most students should find Sample A significantly stronger. Discuss differences between A and B, asking students to comment on what makes A stronger. Where does the Sample B writer go off-track? (Note our suggested revision.)

Step 4: Modeling Revision

- Share Sample C (*Whole Class Revision*) with students. Read it aloud.
- Identify the main focus of the passage: *What is the writer's main point?*
- Ask students whether the writer sticks to this main point the whole time. (Most students should say *no*.) With students' help, identify those places where the author seems to go off track. If students agree a sentence could be deleted, draw a line through it.
- When you finish, read your revised passage aloud, checking for focus. (Compare your revised version with ours, if you wish.)

Step 5: Revising with Partners

- Share Sample D (*Revising with Partners*). Ask students to follow the basic steps you modeled with Sample C. *Working with partners*, they should:
- Read the whole passage through (aloud) to get a sense of the main focus.
- Cross out sentences that seem off-focus.
- Read the result aloud to hear the impact of the revision.

Step 6: Sharing and Discussing Results

- When students have finished, ask several pairs of students to share their revisions aloud and discuss what they deleted and why. Emphasize the importance of keeping the focus clear and strong, not trying to tell *two stories* or make *two main points* at the same time.

Next Steps

- Remind students to create rough drafts with double- or triple-spaced copy to make revision easier.

- As soon as possible following this lesson, ask students to revise a piece of their own writing for focus. Suggest that students begin with a simple revision strategy: delete what does not fit (by crossing it out).

■ Published writers *usually* (though not always!) make clear connections between ideas. A good way to test this is to ask students, "What is the main idea of this passage?" Having the writer's main idea clearly in mind (even if the writer is yourself) is the first step in determining what other supporting ideas are connected. Ask "What is the main idea here?" when sharing literature aloud. Recommended:

  ● *Because of Winn-Dixie* by Kate DiCamillo. 2000. Cambridge, MA: Candlewick Books.

  ● *Creepy Creatures* by Sneed B. Collard III. 1997. Watertown, MA: Charlesbridge.

  ● *Jellies* by Twig George. 2001. Minneapolis: Millbrook Press.

  ● *Seahorses* by Twig George. 2003. Minneapolis: Millbrook Press.

■ *For students who need a challenge:* Sometimes, ideas really *are* connected in the writer's mind—but not in the writing itself. A writer doesn't always realize this, however, until he or she reads the writing aloud. Ask students to share their own writing aloud with partners, listening for any details or examples that do not seem connected to the main message. Discuss the connection—then revise by deleting unrelated information or making the connection clear.

Sample A

The tiny ruby-throated hummingbird might be only three inches long, but it can make a lot of noise. When a hummingbird flies, it makes a loud buzzing sound that comes from its wings beating 60 times a second. You will almost always hear a hummingbird coming!

Sample B

Some birds are huge. The ostrich, which stands over six feet high, is the biggest of them all. Some buildings are also large, and animals such as the elephant are huge, too. The ostrich lays gigantic eggs with a thick shell. Predators like snakes cannot get through that shell easily. Elephants enjoy the water and take a lot of baths in hot weather. So do hippos. Some people actually eat ostriches—and many people eat their eggs!

Suggested Revision of Sample B

Some birds are huge. The ostrich, which stands over six feet high, is the biggest of them all. ~~Some buildings are also large, and animals such as the elephant are huge, too.~~ The ostrich lays gigantic eggs with a thick shell. Predators like snakes cannot get through that shell easily. ~~Elephants enjoy the water and take a lot of baths in hot weather. So do hippos.~~ Some people actually eat ostriches—and many people eat their eggs!

Sample C: Whole Class Revision

Vitamins are important to good health. We get vitamins from foods like salad, fresh fruit, fish, nuts, and grains like oatmeal. One of the best ways to cook fish is outside on the grill. It is important to keep fresh food in the refrigerator. Otherwise, it can lose its vitamins.

Sample D: Revising with Partners

Many people know that whales make a kind of "music."

They sing to each other. They seem to like other music,

too. Once when Beluga whales were trapped in freezing

water between Russia and Alaska, some rescuers

played classical music. The whales followed the music

to safety! Lots of people like music. Some people enjoy

dancing, too!

Suggested Revisions of C and D

Sample C: Whole Class Revision

Vitamins are important to good health. We get vitamins from foods like salad, fresh fruit, fish, nuts, and grains like oatmeal. ~~One of the best ways to cook fish is outside on the grill.~~ It is important to keep fresh food in the refrigerator. Otherwise, it can lose its vitamins.

Sample D: Revising with Partners

Many people know that whales make a kind of "music." They sing to each other. They seem to like other music, too. Once when Beluga whales were trapped in freezing water between Russia and Alaska, some rescuers played classical music. The whales followed the music to safety! ~~Lots of people like music. Some people enjoy dancing, too!~~

Matching Subjects and Verbs

Trait Connection: **Conventions**

Introduction (Share with students in your own words)

When writers work too fast, sometimes they do not realize that their subjects and verbs do NOT go together. Reading aloud can help a writer catch mismatches like these:

The elephants <u>is</u> hungry.

They <u>was</u> my friends.

The elephants *is* hungry—or The elephants *are* hungry? Which one sounds right? If you said *are*, you're spot on. They *was* my friends? Or—They *were* my friends? If you said *were*, you're editing like a pro today. Here's how to use the caret and delete sign to correct our faulty sentences:

The elephants ~~is~~ hungry.
are

They ~~was~~ my friends.
were

Teaching the Lesson (General Guidelines for Teachers)

1. Practice correcting several subject-verb mismatches, using the caret and delete symbol. (Use our sample sentences, or make up your own.)

2. Share the editing lesson on the following page. Students should read the passage aloud, looking and listening for subject-verb mismatches.

3. Ask them to work individually first, then check with a partner.

4. When everyone is done, ask them to coach you as you edit the copy on an overhead transparency, using the caret and delete symbol.

5. When you finish, compare your revision to our suggestion on page 59.

Editing Goal: Catch 4 or more errors (out of 6).
Then, look for subject-verb mismatches in your own work.

Editing Practice

Making Subjects & Verbs Match

Ants is interesting creatures. They works hard
all day long! They build long tunnels in the ground,
where they lives. There are thousands of ants in
one colony. They all has different jobs. Some take
care of the eggs. Some go out to look for food.
They is all important. The most important ant of all
is the Queen Ant. She does not work like the other
ants. She just lay eggs!

Edited Copy

Matching Subjects & Verbs
6 errors corrected

Ants ~~is~~ (are) interesting creatures. They ~~works~~ (work) hard

all day long! They build long tunnels in the ground,

where they ~~lives~~ (live). There are thousands of ants in

one colony. They all ~~has~~ (have) different jobs. Some take

care of the eggs. Some go out to look for food.

They ~~is~~ (are) all important. The most important ant of all

is the Queen Ant. She does not work like the other

ants. She just lay (s) eggs!

Revising the Lead

Trait Connection: **Organization**

Introduction

A good lead does just what its name says. It "leads" a reader into the writing by making a piece of writing sound irresistible. Did you ever see a movie trailer (preview), and think to yourself, "I've just got to see that movie!"? Good leads work the same way. Would this one make you keep reading? "This will be a report about the King Cobra." No? Well, how about this one: "The King Cobra is one of the deadliest snakes on the planet." If you said that one was better, you've got a good ear for leads. In this lesson, you will have a chance to revise some leads that need your help.

Teacher's Sidebar . . .

There is no formula for writing a good lead. A question might work well sometimes—but it is not *always* the best lead. A startling fact can grab a reader's attention, but so might a comment from a character. Leads are as different as the people who write them. And as your students will discover with practice, a good lead can be just a few words long—or it might go on for several sentences.

Focus and Intent

This lesson is intended to help students:

- Understand the importance of a good lead.
- Distinguish between effective and lackluster leads.
- Develop skills in revising a lead that needs work.

Teaching the Lesson

Step 1: Introducing the Idea of a Strong Lead

Begin by imagining that you are going to write a story on any topic: e.g., *the day I got my new kitten*. (This is only an example. Make up your own story based on something that *really happened to you*. Keep it *short*.) Tell your story *within a minute or less*, and then ask students to help you brainstorm several leads you could use for this story if you were to write it. Add some possible leads of your own to the list, including one or two you *definitely do not* consider strong. Talk about what makes a lead work well.

Less effective leads

- This will be the story of how I got my new kitten Murphy.
- I want to tell you about my new kitten Murphy.
- Do you like kittens? I do, too. Here's the story of one kitten.

More effective leads

- The moment I saw Murphy I knew he was the kitten for me.
- Murphy wasn't the most beautiful kitten I had ever seen—but he was definitely the most comical.

Step 2: Making the Reading-Writing Connection

Share the following suggested sample from literature, or any other favorite lead(s) of your own. Ask students whether this (or any) lead makes them want to keep reading, and what questions it raises in their minds:

Sample

You might want to know why I did what I did.

(Lauren Child, *Clarice Bean Spells Trouble*. 2004. Cambridge, MA: Candlewick Press, page 5.)

Step 3: Involving Students as Evaluators

Ask students to review Samples A and B, specifically considering the lead: Will it get readers' attention? Does it offer a clue about what will come next or make you want to keep reading? Have students work with a partner, underlining the lead, and making notes or highlighting any parts of the passage a writer might use to create a stronger lead (e.g., an interesting or unusual detail that comes later in the writing).

Discussing Results

Most students should find Sample B significantly stronger. Discuss differences between A and B, asking students to comment on other ways the author of Sample A might have begun. Possible alternatives to Sample A are provided if you wish to share them.

Step 4: Modeling Revision

- Share Sample C (*Whole Class Revision*) with students. Read the whole passage aloud. Then, read *just the lead*. Underline it.
- Talk about whether the lead is effective. (Most students will likely say *no*.) Make a list of two or three (or more) possible revisions, and choose the class favorite.

■ When you finish, read your revised passage aloud, including your students' favorite lead. (You may compare your revised version with ours, keeping in mind that *their chosen lead does not need to match ours*.)

Step 5: Revising with Partners

Share Sample D (*Revising with Partners*). Ask students to follow the basic steps you modeled with Sample C. *Working with partners*, they should:

■ Read the whole passage aloud.

■ Underline the existing lead.

■ Look through the whole passage to get ideas for alternate leads.

■ Write one or more revisions, using information from the passage—or their imaginations.

Step 6: Sharing and Discussing Results

When students have finished, ask several pairs of students to share their new leads and talk about what makes each effective. (Feel free to share our suggested revision, presenting it as "one possibility," not "the answer.") Emphasize originality and the capacity of each lead to pull the reader into the piece.

Next Steps

■ Continue to identify favorite leads from literature—as well as newspapers, magazines, brochures, advertisements—*anything in print*. Recommended:

- *Clarice Bean Spells Trouble* by Lauren Child. 2004. Cambridge, MA: Candlewick Press.

- *Charlotte's Web* by E. B. White. 1952 (renewed 1980). New York: HarperCollins.

- *Click, Clack, Moo: Cows That Type* by Doreen Cronin. 2000. New York: Simon & Schuster.

- *How to Fish for Trouble (Willimena Rules!)* by Valerie Wilson Wesley. 2004. New York: Hyperion.

- *The Remarkable Benjamin Franklin* by Cheryl Harness. 2005. Washington, D. C.: National Geographic.

■ As soon as possible following this lesson, ask students to create two (or more) leads for any piece of their own writing, then to share their leads with a partner or in a response group to see which one listeners find most effective.

■ *For students who need a challenge:* It is hard to write a lead out of nothing. Suggest that students write a rough draft lead to get started, then revise the lead *after their draft is finished*. Often, details from within the text itself provide good material for a revised lead.

Sample A

Cell phones are interesting. The first cell phones were so big they were kept in cars as car phones. Now most are tiny. They used to be gray or black, but now they come in just about any color. In the 1980s, most cell phone users lived in the U.S. Now, you can call almost any country on your cell.

Sample B

A butterfly does not begin its life with wings. It does not even begin with legs! It starts as an egg. When the egg hatches, a caterpillar emerges. The caterpillar spends its life eating, eating, eating. When it is full grown, it forms a cocoon-like structure called a chrysalis. It lives inside the chrysalis for weeks or months, changing into a totally different creature: the butterfly!

Suggested Revisions of Sample A

Cell phones ~~are interesting.~~ *have really changed!* The first cell phones were so big they were kept in cars as car phones. Now most are tiny. They used to be gray or black, but now they come in just about any color. In the 1980s, most cell phone users lived in the U.S. Now, you can call almost any country on your cell.

Sample C: Whole Class Revision

Do you like giraffes? I do. Let me tell you why. At 18 feet, giraffes are the tallest land animals. They also have the longest necks of any animal. A giraffe's heart has to pump blood up that long neck and bring it back up the giraffe's tall legs. A long neck can be a good thing, though. With their long necks, giraffes can reach leaves from the highest trees!

Sample D: Revising with Partners

The warthog is a kind of animal. The warts are like thick calluses on the animal's head. They protect the warthog during fights. Unless they're cornered, warthogs do not fight, though. They run away from lions, leopards, and hyenas. Warthogs do not need to fight for food because they eat mostly grasses, roots, and berries.

Suggested Revisions of C and D

Sample C: Whole Class Revision

A giraffe needs a very strong heart. Here's why. ~~Do you like giraffes? I do. Let me tell you why.~~ At 18 feet, giraffes are the tallest land animals. They also have the longest necks of any animal. A giraffe's heart has to pump blood up that long neck and bring it back up the giraffe's tall legs. A long neck can be a good thing, though. With their long necks, giraffes can reach leaves from the highest trees!

Sample D: Revising with Partners

gets its name from four thick calluses found on its head. The warthog ~~is a kind of animal.~~ The warts ~~are like thick calluses on the animal's head. They~~ protect the warthog during fights. Unless they're cornered, warthogs do not fight, though. They run away from lions, leopards, and hyenas. Warthogs do not need to fight for food because they eat mostly grasses, roots, and berries.

Cutting Down on Exclamation Points

Trait Connection: **Conventions**

Introduction (Share with students in your own words)

It is easy to get carried away with exclamation points, using one after every sentence—or even more than one!!! This might be all right in a note or e-mail to a friend, but in most writing, it is exclamation point *overload*. One per paper is a good rule. If you feel you need more, it could be time to change the wording:

Boris was running really fast down the road!

The writer could just delete this exclamation point. But sometimes a better choice is to find a stronger way to say the same thing:

Boris was *racing* down the road.

Teaching the Lesson (General Guidelines for Teachers)

1. Practice eliminating exclamation points by just replacing them with periods *or* by changing the wording so the writing is stronger.

2. Share the editing lesson on the following page. Students should read the passage aloud, asking themselves which exclamation points could be removed.

3. Ask them to work individually first, then check with a partner.

4. When everyone is done, ask them to coach you as you edit the same copy, deleting exclamation points (replacing them with periods) and—possibly—changing the wording (optional).

5. When you finish, compare your edited copy to ours, page 71.

Editing Goal: Delete at least 7 (of 9) exclamation points.
Next, look for places to cut down on exclamation marks in your own work.

Editing Practice

Cutting Down on Exclamation Points

It was the big day! Our team, the Wild Cats, was having a race against another team, the Panthers! We were very excited and nervous! The race was the first day of June, and it was hot! We had been practicing, running every single day, so we were ready! The whistle blew, and we were off! At first, the Panthers had a big lead! Then three of our runners pulled ahead! We had won!

Edited/Revised Copy

Cutting Down on Exclamation Points

It was the big day. Our team, the Wild Cats,

was having a race against another team, the

Panthers. We were ~~very~~ _extremely_ excited and nervous.

The race was the first day of June, and it

was _scorching_ hot. We had been practicing, running

every single day, so we were _more than_ ready. The

whistle blew, and we ~~were off!~~ _took off like rockets!_ At first, the

Panthers had a ~~big~~ _huge_ lead. Then three of our

runners pulled ahead. We had won!

Revising the Conclusion

Trait Connection: **Organization**

Introduction

When you finish talking to a friend on the phone, what happens? Do you just hang up? No—probably, you say goodbye. A good conclusion is a way of saying good-bye to your reader. A conclusion wraps up a discussion or story—and sometimes reveals something important the writer has learned—or is still wishing for. In this lesson, you will practice revising endings so they say goodbye to the reader without just "hanging up."

Teacher's Sidebar . . .

Writers may end with a last thought, a surprise, a description, a revealed secret, a comment from a character, a question—or in any of a hundred other ways. What counts is leaving the reader with something to think about. Good conclusions sometimes look back to emphasize an important point—but they do not simply repeat what has already been said. A good conclusion offers the reader a new way of looking at things, or (best of all) makes the reader wish the piece would go on for a few more pages!

Focus and Intent

This lesson is intended to help students:

- Understand the importance of a good conclusion.
- Distinguish between effective and ho-hum conclusions.
- Develop skills in revising a conclusion that needs work.

Teaching the Lesson

Step 1: Introducing the Idea of a Strong Conclusion

Return to the story you told students to open Lesson 8: e.g., *The day I picked out my new kitten.* (This was *our example from that lesson.* Obviously yours is different. Take a minute to remind yourself of the story you used previously.) Refresh your students' memories about the story and the lead you chose together. Write that lead on an overhead so they can refer to it. Then, tell them you want to end your story with the same punch. List some *possible* ways to end (asking students for other suggestions): e.g.,

- something you learned
- something you'll do differently in the future
- a striking image
- a quotation from you or another character in your story

Using these or other possibilities your students think of, brainstorm up to three (or even more) ways you could end your story. Choose your favorite:

- *Who knew Murphy would become my best friend?*
- *A cat who isn't beautiful on the outside can still have a big heart.*
- *His eyes always seem to say, "I'm a pest, but I'm lovable."*

Step 2: Making the Reading-Writing Connection

Share the following suggested sample from literature, or any other favorite conclusion(s) from your reading. Ask students if they think this or any conclusion has its own special sound and feeling—like the writer is saying "Goodbye" for now:

Sample

You see, sometimes things are hard to explain.
Sometimes things that go wrong also go right.
And sometimes your bad luck just has to turn good.

(Lauren Child, *Clarice Bean Spells Trouble*. 2004. Cambridge, MA: Candlewick Press, page 189.)

Step 3: Involving Students as Evaluators

Ask students to review Samples A and B, specifically considering the conclusion: Which one is stronger? Which one seems to wrap up the discussion more effectively? Have students work with a partner, making notes about how each conclusion makes them *feel* as a reader.

Discussing Results

Most students should find Sample B significantly stronger. Discuss differences between A and B, asking students to comment on how each conclusion affects them as readers. A possible alternative to Sample A is provided if you wish to share it.

Step 4: Modeling Revision

- Share Sample C (*Whole Class Revision*) with students. Read the whole passage aloud. Then, read *just the conclusion*. Underline it.
- Talk about whether the conclusion is effective. (Most students should say *no*.) Make a list of two or three (or more) possible revisions, and choose the class favorite.
- When you finish, read your revised passage aloud, including your students' favorite conclusion. (You may compare your revised version with ours, keeping in mind that *their conclusion does not need to match ours*.)

Step 5: Revising with Partners

Share Sample D (*Revising with Partners*). Ask students to follow the basic steps you modeled with Sample C. *Working with partners*, they should:

- Read the passage aloud.
- Underline the existing conclusion.
- Look carefully through the whole passage to get ideas for alternate conclusions.
- Write one or more revisions, based on the passage or on their imaginations.

Step 6: Sharing and Discussing Results

When students have finished, ask several pairs of students to share their new conclusions. Talk about what makes each effective. (Feel free to share our suggested revision, presenting it as "one possibility.") Emphasize the importance of *wrapping up the story or discussion*.

Next Steps

- We think Sample B from this lesson has a fairly strong conclusion. Your students may feel they can improve it, though. If so, let them try!

- Continue to identify favorite conclusions from literature. Listen for the ending as you read. It really *does* have a special sound and feeling. Notice endings to individual chapters within a book. How do endings link a previous chapter to the one coming up? How do endings echo an idea suggested in the lead? Recommended:
  - *Clarice Bean Spells Trouble* by Lauren Child. 2004. Cambridge, MA: Candlewick Press
  - *Diary of a Spider* by Doreen Cronin. 2005. New York: HarperCollins.
  - *A Frog Thing* by Eric Drachman. 2005. Los Angeles: Kidwick Books.
  - *Nothing Ever Happens on 90th Street* by Roni Schotter. 1997. New York: Scholastic.

- As soon as possible following this lesson, ask students to create two (or more) conclusions for any piece of their *own writing*, then to share their conclusions with a partner or in a response group to see which one listeners find more effective.

- Continue the practice of creating at least two conclusions for any original piece. Ask students to think about the connection between the lead and the conclusion.

- *For students who need a challenge:* Collect some leads and conclusions (three sets or more) from favorite literature. Write each on a sentence strip or 3×5 card. See if students can pair up the leads and conclusions that go together—and explain how they connect.

Sample A

A pet takes a lot of work and time. Even a simple goldfish has to be fed. It also needs the water in its bowl or tank cleaned. A dog takes more work. It has to be fed, groomed, and exercised. Cats also need attention and love. In summary, a pet takes a lot of work and time.

Sample B

Frogs are not all alike. Some are poisonous. Some climb trees. Some are as small as your thumbnail, while others grow as large as footballs! Frogs might be fun to look at, but remember, they need fresh water and <u>live</u> food! So when you see one outdoors, don't take it home. Frogs do not make good pets!

Suggested Revision of Sample A

A pet takes a lot of work and time. Even a

simple goldfish has to be fed. It also needs

the water in its bowl or tank cleaned. A dog

takes more work. It has to be fed, groomed,

and exercised. Cats also need attention and

love. ~~In summary, a pet takes a lot of work~~ ᵃ

~~and time.~~ ᵃ^ Before you decide on a pet, find out how much time you will need to spend caring for it. That way, you won't wind up wishing you were pet-free!

Note
This revised conclusion builds on information from the passage without simply saying the same thing over again. It guides the reader's thinking to the "next step."

Sample C: Whole Class Revision

A yo-yo is made of two disks joined together. String is wound around the middle, so it looks like a big, flat spool of thread. By holding onto the string and flicking your wrist, you can make the yo-yo spin out, then return to your hand. People who get really good at yo-yo tricks compete in an annual contest in California. In conclusion, the yo-yo is a fun toy.

Sample D: Revising with Partners

Last summer, my friend Ben invited me to go swimming. It was my first time swimming in a lake. They had a floating dock and when I jumped from it, my feet could not touch the bottom. I panicked! I swallowed about a gallon of water. I could see Ben jumping up and down. He was yelling, but I couldn't hear him. He threw me an inner tube. I caught it and floated in to shore. So everything turned out OK.

Suggested Revisions of C and D

Sample C: Whole Class Revision

A yo-yo is made of two disks joined together. String is wound around the middle, so it looks like a big, flat spool of thread. By holding onto the string and flicking your wrist, you can make the yo-yo spin out, then return to your hand. People who get really good at yo-yo tricks compete in an annual contest in California. ~~In conclusion, the yo-yo is a fun toy.~~ Who would think a game that looks so simple could be so challenging?

Sample D: Revising with Partners

Last summer, my friend Ben invited me to go swimming. It was my first time swimming in a lake. They had a floating dock and when I jumped from it, my feet could not touch the bottom. I panicked! I swallowed about a gallon of water. I could see Ben jumping up and down. He was yelling, but I couldn't hear him. He threw me an inner tube. I caught it and floated in to shore. ~~So everything turned out OK.~~ Even though I got scared, I had fun, and I am going back!

Putting It Together
(Lessons 1, 3, 5, 7, & 9)

Trait Connection: **Conventions**

Introduction (Share with students in your own words)

Editors get better with practice. In this lesson, you'll have a chance to combine skills from several practice lessons. You will be inserting missing letters or words, crossing out repeated words, making sure subjects and verbs match, and cutting down on the number of exclamation points in the copy. Can you do all those things at the same time? Absolutely! Here goes.

Teaching the Lesson (General Guidelines for Teachers)

1. Begin by reviewing the caret and delete symbol. Make sure all students are comfortable using these marks and know what they mean.

2. Review the importance of watching for missing or repeated letters and words.

3. Review the need for subjects and verbs to match: e.g., They *are*, not They *is*.

4. Review the importance of keeping exclamation points to a minimum in any one piece. One is usually enough!

5. Share the editing lesson on the following page. Students should read the passage aloud, looking *and listening* for things they wish to change.

6. Ask them to work individually first, then check with a partner.

7. When everyone is done, ask them to coach you as you edit the same copy, making any changes you and they decide are important. Be sure to use carets and delete symbols as you work.

8. When you finish, compare your edited copy to the one on page 83.

Editing Goal: Correct 8 (or more) of 10 errors;
delete 7 (or more) of 9 exclamation points.
Next, look for editorial changes needed in your own work.

Editing Practice

- **Missing letters or words**
- **Repeated letters or words**
- **Matching subjects and verbs**
- **Too many exclamation points**

Have you ever planted garden? I have! Firs,

you need a patch of ground. You also needs seeds!

Dig up the the soil until it crumble in your hand.

Smooth the soil with rake. The, use a string to to

make a a straight line. Along the line, punch in holes

about an inch deep! Put one or two seeds in in each

hole! Cover them up! Water the seeds lightly! Don't

use too much water or you might drown them! Soon

you wil have plants!

Edited Copy

10 errors corrected
7 of 8 exclamation points cut (Your total may differ.)

Have you ever planted garden? I have. First,

you need a patch of ground. You also needs seeds.

Dig up the the soil until it crumbles in your hand.

Smooth the soil with rake. Then use a string to to

make a straight line. Along the line, punch in holes

about an inch deep. Put one or two seeds in in each

hole. Cover them up. Water the seeds lightly. Don't

use too much water or you might drown them! Soon

you will have plants.

Note
When editing with students, look for errors
first. Then, go back to consider exclamation
points. We have marked periods (to replace
exclamation points) as an editor does: a bold
dot with a circle around it.

Revising the Order

Trait Connection: **Organization**

Introduction

Good writers go back and read what they have written (aloud!) to see if it makes sense. That's what you'll do in this lesson—only you'll be working with someone *else's* writing. Putting *someone else's* written text in order is not *quite* the same as organizing your own writing, but it is very good practice.

Teacher's Sidebar . . .
When you read a passage aloud, your ears will tell you whether it's easy to follow and makes sense. You can also look *and* listen for small **clues,** like repeated words and ideas or connecting words (*Next, Later, For example, In addition*) that guide you right down the path of the writer's thinking.

Focus and Intent

This lesson is intended to help students:

- Understand the importance of clear organization.
- Distinguish between clear and confusing order.
- Put sentences in an order that makes sense.

Teaching the Lesson

Step 1: Introducing the Idea of Order

Begin simply, with just three or four sentences. Let students know you will be giving them several sentences out of order. Read them aloud together, and ask students if they can put the sentences into an order that makes sense. Use the following example or create one of your own based on a topic your class is currently studying. (Use *no more than four* sentences for this warm-up.)

1. It could not be just any old dog, though.
2. She wanted it more than anything.
3. Eliki wanted a dog.
4. It had to have black fur and a bushy tail.

Invite students to discuss possibilities with a partner, then to come up with the order they think makes the most sense. (We suggest 3, 2, 1, 4.) Talk about little **clues** in the writing (e.g., repeated words, the pronoun *it*) that help a reader put things in order.

Step 2: Making the Reading-Writing Connection

If the following sentences were written out of order, could your students put them back in order? Try it and see. Write them on individual sentence strips (7 strips in all) and see if students can match Judy Blume's order. Then, read the original passage (more than once) so students can listen for the clues that connect ideas (How can you tell when the pronouns *he* or *his* refer to Andrew—and when they refer to Nicky?).

Sample

Andrew Marcus wanted freckles. Nicky Lane had freckles. He had about a million of them. They covered his face, his ears and the back of his neck. Andrew didn't have any freckles. He had two warts on his finger. But they didn't do him any good at all.

(Judy Blume, *Freckle Juice*. 1971. New York: Random House, page 11.)

Step 3: Involving Students as Evaluators

Ask students to review Samples A and B, specifically considering order: Which one seems clear? Which one seems confusing? Have students work with a partner, making notes in the right margin about anything that seems out of place. Encourage them to circle sentences and draw arrows showing how they might move things to improve the organization.

Discussing Results

Most students should find Sample B significantly stronger. Discuss differences between A and B, asking students how they might revise A to improve the organization. One alternative to Sample A is provided.

Step 4: Modeling Revision

- Share Sample C (*Whole Class Revision*) with students. Read it aloud.
- Talk about whether the order is easy to follow. (Most students should say *no.*) Invite students to coach you through a class revision, numbering sentences to show how you would re-order them. ***Add transitional phrases as needed*** (see revised Sample A) to make the piece read smoothly.
- When you finish, read the sentences aloud in order. Is the organization easier to follow? (Compare your revised version with ours.)

Step 5: Revising with Partners

Share Sample D (*Revising with Partners*). Ask students to follow the basic steps you modeled with Sample C. *Working with partners*, they should:

- Read all the sentences aloud.
- Discuss the order.

- Revise by renumbering sentences, and (if needed) ***adding transitional phrases*** to make the flow smooth.

- (Optional) Recopy text with sentences in order.

- Read the revised copy aloud to make sure it makes sense.

Step 6: Sharing and Discussing Results

When students have finished, ask several pairs of students to share their newly ordered sentences aloud. How many students came up with the same order? (Point out that our suggested revision is "one possibility," not "the answer." However, any revision *must make sense*.) Emphasize the importance of *reading aloud* when revising for organization.

Next Steps

- Use ideas from previous lessons (stronger leads, conclusions) to make further revisions to any samples from this lesson.

- Encourage students to read their own drafts aloud to "test" the organization. Encourage them to try different possibilities before making a decision.

- Take any 5-sentence (or longer) piece from a published work and print it out in individual sentence strips. Shuffle them and ask students, in pairs or groups, to try putting them back in order. The better the organization of the original piece, the easier this task will be. Recommended:
  - *Freckle Juice* by Judy Blume. 1971. New York: Random House.
  - *George and Martha* by James Marshall. 2000. Boston: Houghton Mifflin. [Divide into paragraphs, rather than single sentences.]
  - *Next Stop Neptune* by Alvin Jenkins. 2004. Boston: Houghton Mifflin. [Choose individual paragraphs.]
  - *On the Wing: Bird Poems and Paintings* by Douglas Florian. 1996. Orlando: Harcourt. [Choose a short 4-6-line poem.]
  - *Tornado* by Stephen Kramer. 1992. Minneapolis: Carolrhoda Books. [Choose short paragraphs of 5 or 6 sentences.]

- *For students who need a challenge:* Invite a student volunteer to print out his or her own writing in individual sentence strips and to "test" the organization by asking class members to try putting the strips in order. Is it easy or hard? Does their response match the writer's original? If not, ask the writer to talk about whether he/she might consider (1) reorganizing the piece, or (2) making the original organization more clear.

Sample A

Rats are also playful and ticklish. Some pet owners even say they have heard their pet rats laugh! Most people think rats are filthy and sneaky. They are often blamed for carrying disease. People who keep rats as pets, however, say that rats are clever. They're so smart it is hard to find a cage they can't open.

Hint
Start by figuring out where the piece begins.

Sample B

It is said no two snowflakes are alike, but since there are so many, it is impossible to know for sure. We can't look at every flake, but scientists *can* measure snowfall in inches. The biggest annual snowfall ever recorded was on Mt. Baker in Washington State. Mt. Baker got 1140 inches during the late 1990s. That is a LOT of flakes—especially when we know they are all different!

Suggested Revision of Sample A

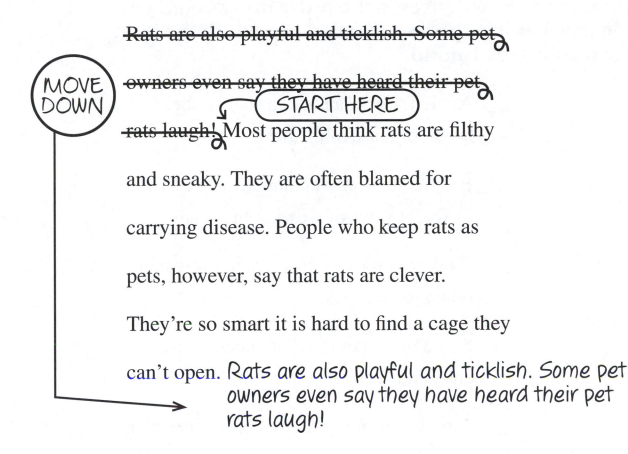

~~Rats are also playful and ticklish. Some pet~~ ~~owners even say they have heard their pet~~

MOVE DOWN

START HERE

~~rats laugh!~~ Most people think rats are filthy

and sneaky. They are often blamed for

carrying disease. People who keep rats as

pets, however, say that rats are clever.

They're so smart it is hard to find a cage they

can't open. Rats are also playful and ticklish. Some pet owners even say they have heard their pet rats laugh!

Sample C: Whole Class Revision

**Number the 5 sentences in the order they *should* go.
Add any words or phrases needed to smooth the flow.
Rewrite and read aloud.**

_____ Ancient Egyptians often shaved their
heads because of the heat.

_____ People in different cultures have many
different ways of wearing their hair.

_____ It takes almost seven years to grow hair
down to your waist.

_____ Some never cut it, while others prefer to
shave it all off.

_____ A person wanting to grow his or her hair
out might like to know that it grows
about 1.5 centimeters a month.

Sample D: Revising with Partners

**Number the 9 sentences in the order they *should* go.
Add any words or phrases needed to smooth the flow.
Rewrite and read aloud.**

_____ The first time I tried cooking by myself, everything went wrong.

_____ Oops! I dropped one egg on the floor!

_____ I was going to make scrambled eggs.

_____ First, I put some butter in a pan to melt.

_____ Then, I got out the eggs and cracked them into a bowl.

_____ By the time I got the egg cleaned up off the floor the butter had burned.

_____ I got out more eggs and more butter.

_____ Finally, I had scrambled eggs to eat!

_____ This time I didn't drop or burn anything.

Suggested Revisions

Sample C: Whole Class Revision

(1) People in different cultures have many different ways of wearing their hair. (2) Some never cut it, while others prefer to shave it all off. (3) Ancient Egyptians, *for example,* often shaved their heads because of the heat. (4) A person wanting to grow his or her hair out might like to know that it grows about 1.5 centimeters a month. *(5) No wonder* it takes almost seven years to grow hair down to your waist.

Sample D: Revising with Partners

(1) The first time I tried cooking by myself, everything went wrong. (2) I was going to make scrambled eggs. (3) First, I put some butter in a pan to melt. (4) Then, I got out the eggs and cracked them into a bowl. (5) Oops! I dropped one egg on the floor! (6) By the time I got the egg cleaned up off the floor the butter had burned. (7) I got out more eggs and more butter. (8) This time I didn't drop or burn anything. (9) Finally, I had scrambled eggs to eat!

Using Capitals

Trait Connection: **Conventions**

Introduction (Share with students in your own words)

Capital letters are like little signals to a reader. "Pay attention!" they say—"A new sentence is beginning,"—or, "Hey—this is somebody's name." When writers forget capitals, it causes confusion:

> I threw the ball to sunny. she tossed it back to ray.

In these sentences, Sunny and Ray are people, whose names should be capitalized. Because the word *she* begins sentence 2, it also needs a capital letter. Editors mark a capital letter with a triple underscore mark, like this:

> I threw the ball to sunny. she tossed it back to ray.

When you are editing your own text, you might wish to simply write the capital in right over the lower case letter. That's fine. What matters is *catching* those pesky missing capitals!

Teaching the Lesson (General Guidelines for Teachers)

1. Practice turning lower case letters to capitals, both on names and words that begin sentences.

2. Share the editing lesson on the following page. Note that the ONLY errors in this lesson are missing capitals, but they may occur on names *or* on words that begin a sentence. Note: The term *green sea turtle* does <u>not</u> need to be capitalized.

3. Have students work individually first, then check with a partner. They may mark the capitals as they wish.

4. When everyone is done, ask them to coach you as you edit the same copy.

5. When you finish, check your editing against our text, page 95.

Editing Goal: Catch 5 (or more) of 7 missing capitals.
Next, check for missing capitals in your own work.

Editing Practice

Mark capitals using the triple underscore (≡)
OR, writing right over the lowercase letter

sea turtles are hatched from eggs. The mother turtle lays her eggs deep in the sand. once they hatch, the baby turtles scramble to the ocean as fast as they can go. crabs and gulls try to catch the small turtles, but a few make it to safety.

During the next few years, the turtles live mostly on seaweed and sea grass. they can often be seen diving through rough waves for food. Many sea turtles live off the coast of hawaii. Visitors to hawaii see the turtles on the beaches sunning themselves. visitors who snorkel might also see them swimming along the coral reef!

Edited Copy

7 capitals inserted

Sea turtles are hatched from eggs. The mother turtle lays her eggs deep in the sand. Once they hatch, the baby turtles scramble to the ocean as fast as they can go. Crabs and gulls try to catch the small turtles, but a few make it to safety.

During the next few years, the turtles live mostly on seaweed and sea grass. They can often be seen diving through rough waves for food. Many sea turtles live off the coast of Hawaii. Visitors to Hawaii see the turtles on the beaches sunning themselves. Visitors who snorkel might also see them swimming along the coral reef!

Revising for Expression

Trait Connection: **Voice**

Introduction

Expressive writing has voice. Your writing tends to be expressive when you are excited about a topic or when you say things in your very own way—a way that is *different from anyone else's*. Expressive writing pulls readers into writing because they hear *you* behind the words, and they want to join in the excitement. In this lesson, you'll have a chance to revise some rather flat writing to make it expressive.

Teacher's Sidebar . . .

There is no recipe for expressive writing. No one can tell a writer, "Change this word or that word and your writing will have voice." A simple but useful strategy, therefore, is to "say it like you mean it." That could mean being very direct or honest, changing the wording slightly, giving the reader an image or example that makes the writing interesting, or letting the reader know from your tone how much you care about the message. It does *not* mean using the word *very* in every sentence or tacking on endless exclamation points!!!!!!!

Focus and Intent

This lesson is intended to help students:

- Realize that expression enlivens writing.
- Distinguish between tired and expressive writing.
- Revise lifeless writing to give it voice.

Teaching the Lesson

Step 1: Introducing the Concept of Expressiveness

Begin by asking students to find a more expressive way of writing a single sentence. For each example, ask them to think about the strategy they are using (e.g., stronger language, striking image, forceful tone, letting feelings show). Two examples are provided.

1. Sam got mad and left.	1. Sam grabbed his coat and stomped out.
2. My birthday seemed like a long time away.	2. One by one, I counted off the days until my birthday. It felt like *forever*.
3. The spelling test was hard.	3.
4. My room was not neat.	4.

Step 2: Making the Reading-Writing Connection

Share the following sample, or any passage that illustrates expressive writing. What makes it expressive? Do you think that the writer, Bill Nye, is excited about his topic—heat? What clues tell us so? How would he sound if he were not excited at all?

Sample

What does heat feel like? Like a warm blanket, a fever, a cup of cocoa, a scorching hot beach. Ouch! But what is heat? It's energy. Pure energy! And energy, together with matter, is what makes our universe such a happening place.

(Bill Nye. *Bill Nye The Science Guy's Big Blast of Science*. 1993. Mercer Island, WA: TVbooks, Inc., page 41.)

Step 3: Involving Students as Evaluators

Ask students to review Samples A and B, specifically considering voice: Which one is more expressive? Have students work with a partner, underlining any passages that could be revised and making notes in the margin.

Discussing Results

Most students should find Sample A stronger. Discuss differences between A and B, asking students what gives A its voice, and what they might revise in Sample B. One possible revision of Sample B is provided.

Step 4: Modeling Revision

- Share Sample C (*Whole Class Revision*) with students. Read it aloud.
- Talk about whether Sample C has voice or shows expressiveness. (Most students should say *no*.) Invite students to coach you through a class revision, thinking what you might add or change to "say it like you mean it."
- When you finish, read your revision aloud. Do you hear a difference? (Compare your revision with ours, if you wish.)

Step 5: Revising with Partners

Share Sample D (*Revising with Partners*). Ask students to follow the basic steps you modeled with Sample C. *Working with partners*, they should:

- Read the passage aloud.
- Underline words or passages that need more expression.

- Revise those passages to give the piece more voice.
- Read the result aloud to hear the difference.

Step 6: Sharing and Discussing Results

When students have finished, ask several pairs of students to share their revisions aloud. Does each revision sound a little different? If so, good! Celebrate the fact that voice is partly about individuality! Do the writers sound as if they "mean it"? (Feel free to share our suggested revision, keeping in mind that students' revisions need not match ours *in any way*.) Remind students that there are countless ways to make voice expressive: e.g., playful exaggeration, simile (an interesting comparison), examples that might be familiar to a reader, lively or unusual language, a striking image, a forceful tone.

Next Steps

- Encourage students to routinely *read their own writing aloud*, listening for voice and looking for just one or two passages to enliven.

- As you share writing aloud, listen for passages that illustrate strong voice. Make a collection, and continue to talk about the many different strategies writers use to make writing expressive. Keep a running list and post it. Recommended:
  - *Bill Nye The Science Guy's Big Blast of Science* by Bill Nye. 1993. Mercer Island, WA: TVbooks, Inc.
  - *Clarice Bean Spells Trouble* by Lauren Child. 2004. Cambridge, MA: Candlewick Press.
  - *Dear Mrs. LaRue: Letters from Obedience School* by Mark Teague. 2002. New York: Scholastic.
  - *If I Were in Charge of the World and other worries* by Judith Viorst. 1981. New York: Simon & Schuster.
  - *Matilda* by Roald Dahl. 1998. New York: Puffin.

- Remind your students that voice has no rights or wrongs. In the end, it is mostly about being yourself, and the best strategy for that is just to ask, "How would *I* say this, in my own words, in my own way?"

- *For students who need a challenge:* Ask students to rewrite the Bill Nye example from earlier in this lesson to take all the voice *out*. You might present this as, "Let's make Bill sound bored." Then, talk about strategies they used to do this. Surprisingly, writing to take voice *out* is one of the best strategies for increasing students' awareness of how writers put voice *in*.

Sample A

Marla needed a special gift for her sister's birthday. But with only one dollar, what on earth could she buy? When she saw the sign saying "Balloons—99 cents," she could hardly believe her luck. They even had Sara's favorite color: red. She paid the smiling man and ran down the street, feeling as if she were floating. She could already see the smile on Sara's face. Suddenly, she felt . . . *nothing*. She looked at her hand. The string was gone! She whirled around to see her gift growing smaller, smaller, sailing away, over the trees and out of sight into nowhere. Tears stung her eyes.

Sample B

Jorge had made a pizza. It was the first thing

he had cooked by himself. He felt good about

it. He wanted everyone to taste it.

Suggested Revision of Sample B

Jorge had made a ^gigantic, sizzling^ pizza

with everything on top that a pizza lover

could wish for.

It was the first thing he had cooked by

himself and it was the most beautiful

pizza in the universe. He felt ~~good about it.~~ ^pretty proud of himself.^

He ^wanted everyone to taste it.^ gave samples to his mom, his little

brother, his dog, his goldfish, and even a

little sparrow hopping on the window ledge.

They all fainted with happiness when they

tasted it.

Sample C: Whole Class Revision

The car was old. It was ugly. The inside did

not smell good. It did not always start.

Sample D: Revising with Partners

The word "matter" refers to things in the universe. It refers to anything. The word "matter" comes from an old Latin word that means "stuff." It's a handy word.

Suggested Revisions of C and D

Sample C: Whole Class Revision

The car was ^so old, that most of the paint had worn off and it was hard to tell what color it was. It was ~~ugly,~~ dented on both sides and rusty everywhere. ~~The inside did not smell good.~~ You had to hold your nose to get inside. ~~It did not always start.~~ That poor old car just plain refused to start anymore.

Sample D: Revising with Partners

The word "matter" refers to anything ~~things~~ in the universe. ~~It refers to anything~~ from the tiniest speck of dust to the biggest whale in the ocean. The word "matter" comes from an old Latin word that means "stuff." ~~It's a handy word.~~ What a handy word to know!

Look Out for "Me and Ann"

Trait Connection: **Conventions**

Introduction (Share with students in your own words)

Listen! . . . and you might hear "Me," "Him," or "Her" used as sentence subjects. Do these sound familiar?

> *Me and Ann* went to the park.
> *Her and me* are friends.
> *Him and me* both love chocolate.

This is not correct grammar, but it is used so often, it sometimes sounds as if it *is* both correct and natural. Good writers are careful about grammar because they know that it's easy to make a habit of something—even when you know it's not right.

Me and Ann went to the park should really be—what? If you said ***Ann and I went to the park***, you're right on the editing mark today. What about *Her and me are friends*? If you said ***She and I are friends***, you're sailing. One more. What about *Him and me both love chocolate*—? If you said ***He and I both love chocolate***, you're spot on. (And guess what? You're right about the chocolate, too.)

Teaching the Lesson (General Guidelines for Teachers)

1. Share the examples above, or make up your own examples that show the correct way to express a sentence subject.

2. Share the editing lesson on the following page. Students should read the passage aloud, looking and listening for sentence subjects that are incorrect and need to be rewritten. They should cross these out and write the correct copy above, using a caret (^).

3. Ask them to work individually first, then check with a partner.

4. When everyone is done, ask them to coach you as you edit the copy on an overhead transparency, correcting any errors.

5. When you finish, compare your revision to our suggestion on page 107.

Editing Goal: Correct 4 sentence subject errors.
Follow-Up: Be on the lookout for incorrect sentence subjects in your own work.

Editing Practice

Look Out for "Me and Ann"
Correct any sentence subject errors.

Me and my dog Spider play a hide and seek

game. I hide and Spider finds me. Me and my

brother play sometimes, too, but my dog is

better at it! Me and my dog are the best

friends ever. I don't know what I'd do

without him. Me and him make the best

team in the world.

Note
In this and other lessons, it may be necessary to change a
lower case letter to a capital letter as part of your editing.

Edited Copy

Sentence Subjects
4 errors

~~Me and~~ My dog Spider play a hide and seek *and I*

game. I hide and Spider finds me. ~~Me and~~ My *and I*

brother play sometimes, too, but my dog is *and I*

better at it! ~~Me and~~ My dog are the best *and I*

friends ever. I don't know what I'd do

without him. ~~Me and him~~ make the best *He and I*

team in the world.

Revising for Confidence

Trait Connection: **Voice**

Introduction

When a writer is confident, voice soars. One trick for writing with more confidence is to get rid of qualifiers. Qualifiers are little expressions that make you sound as if you're not sure what you're saying is true—expressions like *somewhat, rather, maybe, kind of, sort of, almost, could be,* and so on. Qualifiers make a writer sound as if she is standing on the diving board, but *kind of, sort of, possibly* afraid to jump. In this lesson, you'll have a chance to cross out qualifiers and *kind of, you know,* boost the voice. *Oops.* Make that *boost the voice!*

> ### Teacher's Sidebar . . .
> *Sometimes* qualifiers are needed for clarity. For example, a person might drive *slightly* over the speed limit. Or the temperature might be *a little* below zero. Not everything is absolute. Problems arise when a writer refuses to say *anything* in a direct manner. This isn't *somewhat* confusing and *sort of* annoying. It's confusing and annoying. Period.

Focus and Intent

This lesson is intended to help students:

- Recognize the importance of confidence in writing.
- Identify qualifying words and expressions.
- Revise by eliminating qualifiers to bring out a confident voice.

Teaching the Lesson

Step 1: Introducing Qualifiers

Begin by sharing any or all of the following four sentences, each of which contains one or more qualifying expressions. For each one, ask what words or phrases could be crossed out to make the writing more confident. Reread each sentence to hear the difference without qualifiers.

1. Ruben felt kind of scared when he saw the hungry lion approach.

2. The cheese smelled almost strange. I wasn't totally ready to try it.

3. Rain came down pretty hard. It sort of, you know, crushed the flowers.

4. I was rather thrilled for the most part when I pretty much won the race.

Step 2: Making the Reading-Writing Connection

Share the following sample, or any passage that illustrates confident, qualifier-free writing. How would this passage sound if Bill Nye had built in many qualifying phrases (e.g., *Go kind of wild, fellow scientists*)?

Sample

If one theory is wrong, we can change it. We can refine it. Or, if need be, we can just toss it out and start over. We can move ahead and try to figure things out. It's our nature. And so far, the Scientific Method is the best way we've come up with. Go wild, fellow scientists.

(Bill Nye. *The Science Guy's Big Blast of Science.* 1993. Mercer Island, WA: TVbooks, Inc., page 7.)

Step 3: Involving Students as Evaluators

Ask students to review Samples A and B, specifically considering voice: Which one is more direct and confident? Have students work with a partner, crossing out any qualifying words or phrases that undermine the confident tone.

Discussing Results

Most students should find Sample B stronger. Discuss differences between A and B, asking students what gives B its voice, and what they might cross out to make A stronger. A possible revision of Sample A is provided.

Step 4: Modeling Revision

- Share Sample C (*Whole Class Revision*) with students. Read it aloud.
- Talk about whether it sounds timid or confident. (Most students should say *timid.*) Invite students to coach you through a class revision, crossing out any words or phrases that get in the way of confidence.
- When you finish, read your revised passage aloud. Do you hear a difference? (Compare your revision with ours, if you wish.)

Step 5: Revising with Partners

Share Sample D (*Revising with Partners*). Ask students to follow the basic steps you modeled with Sample C. *Working with partners,* they should:

- Read the passage aloud.

- Cross out qualifying words or phrases that undermine confidence.
- Read the result aloud to hear the improvement.

Step 6: Sharing and Discussing Results

When students have finished, ask several pairs of students to share their revisions aloud. Does each revision sound more confident? (Feel free to share our suggested revision, keeping in mind that we may have deleted more qualifying phrases than students did.)

Next Steps

- Encourage students to routinely read *their own writing aloud,* listening for qualifiers that get in the way of confidence, and crossing them out—unless they're needed to make the passage clear.

- As you share writing aloud, listen for passages that reflect the writer's confidence. Are they qualifier-free? If not, does the writer use qualifiers carefully, only when necessary? Recommended:

  - *Bill Nye the Science Guy's Big Blast of Science* by Bill Nye. 1993. Mercer Island, WA: TVbooks, Inc.

  - *Bill Nye the Science Guy's Great Big Book of Tiny Germs* by Bill Nye. 2005. New York: Hyperion.

  - *Bill Nye the Science Guy's Great Big Dinosaur Dig* by Bill Nye. 2002. New York: Hyperion.

  - *Bones: Our Skeletal System* by Seymour Simon. 2000. New York: Harper Trophy.

- *For students who need a challenge:* Ask students to rewrite the Bill Nye example from earlier in this lesson by putting in *as many qualifiers as possible*: e.g., *kind of, sort of, sometimes, maybe, in some cases, perhaps,* and so on. Share the results aloud with the whole class. What is the effect on the sound of the passage?

Sample A

In a lunar eclipse, the earth kind of gets like between the moon and the sun. When this happens, the earth sort of blocks out the sun's light a little bit and makes kind of a shadow on the moon. You can still just about see a little sliver of light on the edge of the moon. The earth's shadow is pretty much curved. This is how Egyptians figured out that the earth was sort of round in many ways.

Sample B

In ancient times, people thought the sun and other planets were all circling around the earth. Of course, this is not how the Solar System works. We know today that all planets in our Solar System (including Earth) revolve around the sun. The first person to come up with this idea was Copernicus—way back in 1543. Many people who lived then thought Copernicus was crazy. Scientists today, however, believe his original thinking started a major scientific revolution.

Suggested Revision of Sample A

In a lunar eclipse, the earth ~~kind of~~ gets ~~like~~ between the moon and the sun. When this happens, the earth ~~sort of~~ blocks out the sun's light ~~a little bit~~ and makes ~~kind of~~ a shadow on the moon. You can still ~~just about~~ see a little sliver of light on the edge of the moon. The earth's shadow is ~~pretty much~~ curved. This is how Egyptians figured out that the earth was ~~sort of~~ round ~~in many ways~~.

Sample C: Whole Class Revision

Have you ever seen a high definition television picture? It has kind of a sharp, sort of clear picture. When you watch a football game on a high definition TV, it's more or less like being right there. In fact, it almost feels like you are kind of like sitting on the bleachers. It is quite exciting and most of the time, it's pretty realistic, too.

Sample D: Revising with Partners

A goldfish is almost the perfect pet. It is somewhat easy to care for. You don't have to actually feed it very often. For the most part, goldfish are quiet pets, too. They are pretty much tame, so they will sort of swim right up to you, but they don't bite all that much.

Suggested Revisions of C and D

Sample C: Whole Class Revision

Have you ever seen a high definition television picture? It has ~~kind of~~ a sharp, ~~sort of~~ clear picture. When you watch a football game on a high definition TV, it's ~~more or less~~ like being right there. In fact, it ~~almost~~ feels like you are ~~kind of like~~ sitting on the bleachers. It is ~~quite~~ exciting and ~~most of the time, it's pretty~~ realistic, too.

Sample D: Revising with Partners

A goldfish is ~~almost~~ the perfect pet. It is ~~somewhat~~ easy to care for. You don't have to ~~actually~~ feed it very often. ~~For the most part,~~ Goldfish are quiet pets, too. They are ~~pretty much~~ tame, so they will ~~sort of~~ swim right up to you, but they don't bite. ~~all that much.~~

Would of, Could of, Should of

Trait Connection: **Conventions**

Introduction (Share with students in your own words)

We learn to edit with our ears as much as with our eyes. We hear someone say, "I should have," and to our ears it often sounds like "I should *of*." This is especially true if someone speaks quickly. *Of* is not the right word with *could*, *should*, or *would*, however. You don't want to write any of the following:

I could *of* stayed longer.

I would *of* helped you.

I should *of* studied for my test.

Careful writers remember that *would, could,* and *should* require *have*, not *of*:

I could *have* stayed longer.

I would *have* helped you.

I should *have* studied for my test.

Teaching the Lesson (General Guidelines for Teachers)

1. Share the examples above, or make up your own examples to show the correct use of *have* with *could, would,* or *should.*

2. Share the editing lesson on the following page. Students should read the passage aloud, looking and listening for instances where *of* is used instead of *have*. They should cross out *of* and insert *have*, using a caret (^).

3. Ask them to edit individually first, then check with a partner.

4. When everyone is done, ask them to coach you as you edit the copy on an overhead transparency, correcting any errors you find.

5. When you finish, compare your revision to our suggestion on page 119.

Editing Goal: Correct 5 incorrect uses of the word *of*.
Next, be on the lookout for *of* incorrectly used in place of *have* in your own work.

Editing Practice

Could *have,* Would *have,* Should *have*
Correct any errors

I should of studied longer for the spelling test.

I would of, too, if my friend Max hadn't called

me on the phone. I could of just hung up, but

I had not talked to him for three days. So that

seemed rude! We talked for half an hour. I

should of studied more right then, but my

favorite TV show was on. What could I do? If it

had not been for TV and Max getting in the way,

I would of gotten an A in spelling!

Edited Copy

Could have, Would have, Should have
5 errors corrected

I should ~~of~~ *have* studied longer for the spelling test.

I would ~~of~~ *have* too, if my friend Max hadn't called

me on the phone. I could ~~of~~ *have* just hung up, but

I had not talked to him for three days. So that

seemed rude! We talked for half an hour. I

should ~~of~~ *have* studied more right then, but my

favorite TV show was on. What could I do? If it

had not been for TV and Max getting in the way,

I would ~~of~~ *have* gotten an A in spelling!

Revising to Connect

Lesson 18

Trait Connection: **Voice**

Introduction

Good writers make sure the voice in their writing connects with the reader. If you wrote to a friend, for example, you'd probably use a casual voice. "Hey, what's up?" you might say. If you wrote to a local radio station to say you liked the music, though, you might "dress up" your voice a little—in other words, make it more formal. You might say, "I'm a fan of your show," or "I enjoy the music you play." The point is this: When you write *anything*, you need to think about who will read it. Make sure the voice is right for that reader.

Teacher's Sidebar . . .

Voices are not "right" or "wrong" in and of themselves. The question is, "Does the voice fit the moment?" Most people wouldn't wear shorts and running shoes to a job interview. But on the other hand, a tuxedo is equally out of place at a baseball game. The right voice for the situation is the secret. And—while many business people *do* respond positively to an informal or humorous or playful voice, it's best to tread lightly until you know the person.

Focus and Intent

This lesson is intended to help students:

- Recognize that audience influences voice.
- Distinguish between a casual and a business voice.
- Revise to make sure the voice suits the intended reader.

Teaching the Lesson

Step 1: Introducing "the Right Voice"

Begin by sharing the following paired expressions. The one on the left shows what you might write in an e-mail to a friend. The one on the right shows what you might write in a "business" note or e-mail (to the principal, to the manager of a local theater or restaurant). Look at example #1; then fill in the blanks for each set.

"Right voice" for a friend	"Right voice" for a business person
1. What's happening?	1. How are you?
2. Thanks a million zillion!	2. _____
3. _____	3. That is a very good idea.

Step 2: Making the Reading-Writing Connection

Share the following sample e-mail, or any passage that illustrates a business voice. Ask students, "Do you think Mark wrote this note to a personal friend—or is it an online review of a book Mark liked?" How can you tell? What words would be different if the audience changed?

Sample e-mail

The ABC Thesaurus is very helpful. I used it to look up several words for my report on birds. I would recommend it to my friends.

Sincerely,
Mark

Step 3: Involving Students as Evaluators

Ask students to review Samples A and B, specifically considering voice: Which one has the "right voice" for a business e-mail? Have students work with a partner, underlining any words or phrases they think should be revised for a business e-mail.

Discussing Results

Most students should find Sample B more appropriate for a business e-mail. Discuss differences between A and B, asking students what particular words or expressions make A less suitable for a business audience. A possible "business" revision of Sample A is provided.

Step 4: Modeling Revision

- Share Sample C (*Whole Class Revision*) with students. Read it aloud.
- Talk about whether Sample C sounds appropriate for a business e-mail. (Most students should say *no.*) Invite students to coach you through a class revision, crossing out any words or phrases that are not right for a business audience and revising them so they are more appropriate.
- When you finish, read your revised passage aloud. Do you hear a difference? (Compare your revision with ours, if you wish.)

Step 5: Revising with Partners

Share Sample D (*Revising with Partners*). This time, students will revise to give the e-mail the "right voice" for a note *to a friend*. Ask students to follow the basic steps you modeled with Sample C. *Working with partners,* they should:

- Read the passage aloud.

- Cross out words or phrases that they would probably *not* use in an e-mail to a friend, and revise them to make the note more personal and conversational.

- Read the result aloud to hear the change in voice.

Step 6: Sharing and Discussing Results

When students have finished, ask several pairs of students to share their revisions aloud. Does each revision sound more appropriate for an informal e-mail to a friend? (Feel free to share our suggested revision, if you wish. Your students' revisions are likely to differ.)

Next Steps

- Write e-mails or notes (make your own cards, if you like, or use postcards) to friends. Make a list of words or expressions (including emoticons) that are appropriate in an informal note or e-mail that would NOT be quite as appropriate in a business e-mail.

- Ask students to rewrite Mark's note about using an online thesaurus as if they were writing a thank you note to a good friend who had lent them a book. How different does this same basic message sound when written as a personal note (to a different audience)?

- Talk about formal versus informal voice in the writing you share aloud. Ask your students, "Who is probably the audience for this piece?" Sometimes, they will be the intended audience—but sometimes, it will be older (or younger) students or students *and* adults. Virtually any nonfiction piece will have a slightly more formal voice than nonfiction. But some nonfiction writers (Bill Nye is one) manage to be playful even with serious topics. Following are other recommended texts to contrast with most nonfiction:
  - *The Diary of Melanie Martin: Or How I Survived Matt the Brat, Michelangelo and the Leaning Tower of Pizza* by Carol Weston. 2001. New York: Yearling.
  - *Once Upon a Cool Motorcycle Dude* by Kevin O'Malley. 2005. New York: Walker and Company.
  - *The Twits* by Roald Dahl. 2007 (rev ed). New York: Puffin.

- Picturing a reader as you write can help make voice stronger. Invite students to bring in photographs of people to whom they would like to write a note, and have them look at the photos while writing. Talk about the difference it makes to have the face of the reader right in front of you.

- *For students who need a challenge:* Encourage students to write e-mails (or notes) to one or more businesses in your area and to send them. Review them before sending to be sure the voice is appropriate. Share any responses you get.

Sample A

Dear Super Video:

You are so far out! Your movies are

waaaaaaaaaaaay cool! I love it that

you have about a million billion zillion

movies to choose from! Pleeeeeeeeeeeeze,

get more cartoons!!!!!!!!!!!!!!!!!! They rock! ☺

Bye, guys!

Jon

Sample B

Dear San Diego Zoo:

Last week our class came to visit your zoo and had a guided tour. It was fabulous! I loved everything, but the orangutans were my favorites. Thank you for letting us visit your great zoo!

Sincerely,

Emily

Suggested Revision of Sample A

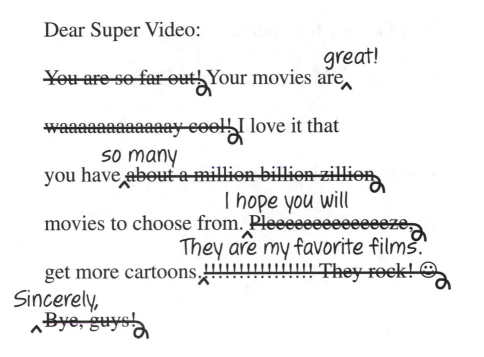

Dear Super Video:

~~You are so far out!~~ Your movies are ^great!

~~waaaaaaaaaaaay cool!~~ I love it that

you have ^so many ~~about a million billion zillion~~

movies to choose from. ~~Pleeeeeeeeeeeeeze,~~ ^I hope you will

get more cartoons. ^They are my favorite films. ~~!!!!!!!!!!!!!!! They rock! ☺~~

Sincerely,

^~~Bye, guys!~~

Jon

Note
The number of exclamation points is drastically reduced.
The emoticon ☺ is deleted, too. It is charming—but informal!

Sample C: Whole Class Revision

Dear Fantasy Ice Cream:

Yo—a big **fat** hello from me! Our field trip to

your company was totally awesome. Dude!

Your ice cream is unreal.

Rock on! ☺

George

Sample D: Revising with Partners

Dear Chris,

Thank you for inviting me to your house last week. I had an excellent time. Your room is very nice. The trip to the park was fun, too.

Let's plan to play again soon.

Sincerely,

K.C.

Suggested Revisions of C and D

Sample C: Whole Class Revision

Dear Fantasy Ice Cream:
Hello from a fan!
~~Yo~~ a big **fat** ~~hello from me!~~ Our field trip to
wonderful.
your company was ~~totally awesome. Dude!~~
delicious.
Your ice cream is ~~unreal.~~
Thank you for the great tour.
~~Rock on! ☺~~
Sincerely,
George

Sample D: Revising with Partners

Dear Chris,
Thanks for the SUPER time!
~~Thank you for inviting me to your house last~~
It was a blast!   awesome. ☺
~~week. I had an excellent time.~~ Your room is
totally ROCKED!!
~~very nice. The trip to~~ The park ~~was fun, too.~~
Call me!!!!!!!!!!!!!!!
~~Let's plan to play again soon.~~
Your bff ;)
~~Sincerely,~~

K.C.

Putting It Together
(Lessons 13, 15, 17)

Trait Connection: **Conventions**

Introduction (Share with students in your own words)

In this lesson, you will have a chance to practice the skills you worked on in Lessons 13, 15, and 17: using capitals for names and for the first word in a sentence; making sure the sentence subject is presented correctly; and making sure to use *have*—not *of*—in *could have, would have, should have*. Does that seem like a lot to remember? You're an editor. You can do it.

Teaching the Lesson (General Guidelines for Teachers)

1. Begin by reviewing strategies and rules applied in Lessons 13, 15, and 17, making sure students feel comfortable with all suggested editorial changes.

2. Pass out the editing lesson on the following page. Students should read the passage aloud, looking *and listening* for things they wish to change.

3. Ask them to edit individually first, then check with a partner.

4. When everyone is done, ask them to coach you as you edit the same copy, making any changes you and they decide are important. Use carets and delete symbols as you work.

5. When you finish, read your edited copy aloud to hear the difference. If you wish, compare your edited version to ours on page 131.

Editing Goal: Correct 6 (or more) of 9 errors.
Next, look for the same kinds of editorial changes needed in your own work.

Editing Practice

- **Capitals**
- **Sentence subjects**
- **Could *have,* not *of***

Me and Pol built an awesome squirrel feeder.

We would of bought one, but we doesn't

have enough money. So him and me just did it

ourselves. It was easy! first, we found some

old lumber no one was using. We nailed some

boards together to make a post. Then pol and

I attached a flat piece to the top. we sank

the post into the ground in a good spot. Then

we put seeds on top. We should of put out even

more food. The squirrels ate it all the very first

night! Me and Pol said that squirrel feeder was

our best project ever.

Edited Copy

9 errors corrected

~~Me and~~ _and I_ Pol built an awesome squirrel feeder.

We would _have_ ~~of~~ bought one, but we ~~doesn't~~ _don't_

have enough money. So ~~him and me~~ _he and I_ just did it

ourselves. It was easy! First, we found some

old lumber no one was using. We nailed some

boards together to make a post. Then Pol and

I attached a flat piece to the top. We sank

the post into the ground in a good spot. Then

we put seeds on top. We should _have_ ~~of~~ put out even

more food. The squirrels ate it all the very first

night! ~~Me and~~ _and I_ Pol said that squirrel feeder was

our best project ever.

Revising for Precision

Trait Connection: **Word Choice**

Introduction

Mark Twain said that the difference between the right word and the *almost* right word was like the difference between *lightning* and *the lightning bug*. The closer a writer comes to saying *precisely* what he or she means (*scrawny Chihuahua* instead of *little dog*), the easier it is for the reader to get the message. In this lesson, you'll look for chances to help writers say *precisely* what they mean.

>
> **Teacher's Sidebar . . .**
> Trading one *single word* for another is not really an efficient way to revise for word choice. Sometimes, you need to cross out a whole phrase or sentence in order to "say it just right."

Focus and Intent

This lesson is intended to help students:

- Understand the importance of precise phrasing.
- Distinguish between precise and vague writing.
- Revise a vague piece to make the wording more precise.

Teaching the Lesson

Step 1: Introducing the Idea of Precision

One easy way to get across the idea of precision is to substitute a specific example for a vague description. Begin by sharing the two examples provided here. Then, with your students, brainstorm precise substitutes for the remaining vague words or phrases in the left column. Invent *any details you need* to make the example precise.

Vague	Precise
small toy	orange yo-yo
made a face at me	squinted his eyes and stuck out his tongue
big animal	_____
bad weather	_____
got upset	_____

Step 2: Making the Reading-Writing Connection

Share the following sample, or any favorite passage that shows precise language. Read it aloud more than once, so students can listen for words or phrases that help them picture the scene in their minds. Imagine if Kate DiCamillo had written *room* instead of "castle library," *came in* instead of "came streaming in," *big openings* instead of "high, tall windows," or had left out the phrase "in bright yellow patches." How effective would the passage have been then? Try it and see.

Sample

Despereaux's sister Merlot took him into the castle library, where light came streaming in through tall, high windows and landed on the floor in bright yellow patches.

(Kate DiCamillo, *The Tale of Despereaux*. 2003. Cambridge, MA: Candlewick Press, page 21.)

Step 3: Involving Students as Evaluators

Ask students to review Samples A and B, specifically considering precision: Which one has more precise language? Which one makes meaning more clear? Have students work with a partner, highlighting words or phrases they like, and underlining anything that needs revision. If they think of a better way to say something, encourage them to scribble it in the right margin.

Discussing Results

Most students should find Sample A significantly stronger. Discuss differences between A and B, asking students how they might revise B to make it more precise. A possible alternative to Sample B is provided.

Step 4: Modeling Revision

■ Share Sample C (*Whole Class Revision*) with students. Read it aloud. Ask whether the word choice is precise. (Most students will likely say *no*.)

■ Invite students to coach you through a class revision, underlining words or phrases you and your students think need more precision.

■ Brainstorm alternatives and write in your favorites. Feel free to cross out phrases or sentences you don't need at all.

■ When you finish, read your revised passage aloud. Is the word choice stronger? (Compare your revision with ours, if you wish.)

Step 5: Revising with Partners

Share Sample D (*Revising with Partners*). Ask students to follow the basic steps you modeled with Sample C. *Working with partners*, they should:

■ Read the passage aloud.

■ Underline words or phrases that could be more precise.

- Revise by substituting new words, phrases, or sentences.
- Read the result aloud to make sure it makes sense.

Step 6: Sharing and Discussing Results

- When students have finished, ask several pairs of students to share their revisions aloud. How many students chose the same words or phrases for revision? (Feel free to share our suggested revision as "one possibility," not "the answer.") Emphasize the impact of revising even *one* vague word or phrase. It may be better to revise three or four, but even one can make a difference!

Next Steps

- We think Sample A from this lesson is fairly strong. If your students feel they can improve the word choice, encourage them to revise it.

- Use ideas from previous lessons (stronger leads or conclusions, additional details) to make further revisions to any samples from this lesson.

- Encourage students to look for even *one word or phrase* in any rough draft (of their own work) that could be revised. Even one makes a difference. Do this routinely as part of revision.

- Listen for precise or unusual language (words, phrases, sentences) in the literature you share aloud. Keep a collection of favorites. Recommended texts with precise language:
  - *The Tale of Despereaux* by Kate DiCamillo. 2003. Cambridge, MA: Candlewick Press.
  - *Crickwing* by Janell Cannon. 2000. New York: Harcourt.
  - *Lord of the Forest* by Caroline Pitcher. 2004. London: Frances Lincoln Children's Books.

- *For students who need a challenge:* Gather a collection of postcards with a variety of pictures—people, animals, scenes. Hand them out and ask students to write one or two sentences describing vividly and precisely what they see. Then, separate pictures from descriptions and shuffle them. See if the class as a whole can match descriptions to the right pictures.

Sample A

Kite flying started thousands of years ago in China. Today's Chinese kites are designed to look like insects, birds, or mythical animals such as dragons. Their light sails are made of paper or silk so they can swirl and dive with the slightest breeze. Kites made of polyester are much heavier. They often droop or crash unless the wind is powerful. Could a kite with broad sails lift a lightweight kite flyer right off his or her toes? You bet! In fact, airplane inventors Wilbur and Orville Wright once tried to fly by hanging onto a kite.

Sample B

Hawks are good hunters. In fact, they
are some of the best hunters. Hawks are
quiet. Their eyesight is about ten times
better than a human's. They can see even
the tiniest things. A hawk is patient. When
its prey shows up, the hawk drops and
picks up the animal in its claws.

Suggested Revision of Sample B

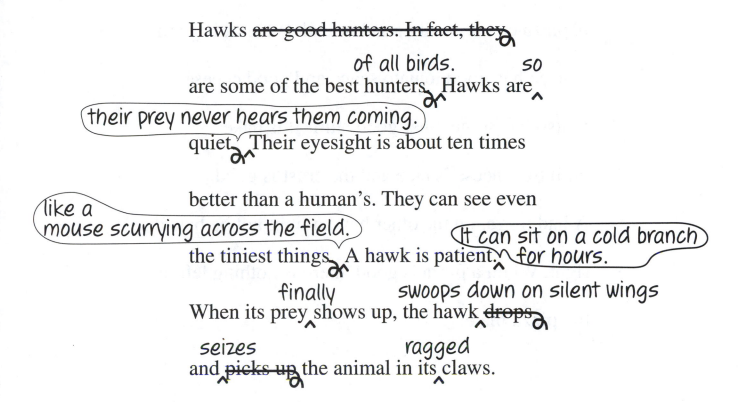

Hawks ~~are good hunters. In fact, they~~ ^a^
                           of all birds.   so
are some of the best hunters. Hawks are ^^
(their prey never hears them coming.) ^a^
        quiet, Their eyesight is about ten times ^a^

(like a
mouse scurrying across the field.)
        better than a human's. They can see even
        the tiniest things, A hawk is patient.^ (It can sit on a cold branch ^^ for hours.) ^a^

                finally   swoops down on silent wings
When its prey shows up, the hawk ~~drops~~ ^a^
        seizes   ragged
and ~~picks up~~ the animal in its claws. ^a^ ^^

Note
Our revision on this piece is fairly extensive. Your students need not revise this heavily. This is only an example to show various possibilities.

Sample C: Whole Class Revision

A pizza can be really good or bad. When it is good,

a pizza has good tomato sauce and good cheese.

It also has some other good stuff. It is baked

until the cheese is nice and the crust is good.

A bad pizza, on the other hand, might not be baked

right. When a pizza is good, there is nothing left on

the pizza plate.

Sample D: Revising with Partners

The weather was bad. In fact, it was

really bad. Rain fell everywhere.

The wind was blowing hard. If this

kept up, we might not be able to hold

our soccer game.

Suggested Revisions of C and D

Sample C: Whole Class Revision

A pizza can be really good or bad. When it is good,

a pizza ~~has good~~ tomato sauce and ~~good~~ cheese. *(is covered with tangy)* *(creamy)*

(is topped with spicy pepperoni and yummy red onions.)

It ~~also has some other good stuff.~~ It is baked

until the cheese is ~~nice~~ and the crust is ~~good.~~ *(golden)* *(crispy.)*

A bad pizza, on the other hand, might ~~not be baked~~ *(be burned or doughy.)*

~~right.~~ When a pizza is good, there is ~~nothing~~ left on *(not one single crumb)*

the pizza plate.

Sample D: Revising with Partners

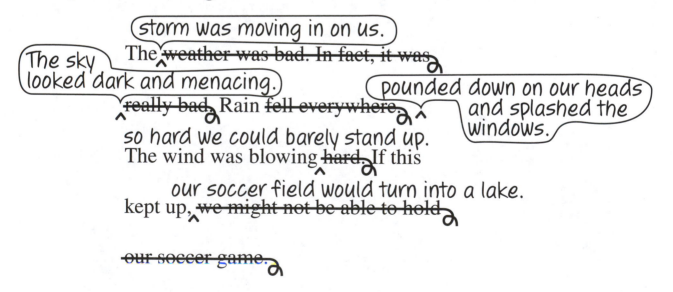

Double Subjects

Trait Connection: **Conventions**

Introduction (Share with students in your own words)

It is fine to write *My brother caught the ball* or *He caught the ball*—but not *My brother he caught the ball*. That's doubling up on subjects. Doubling up is not necessary—and not allowed—when both subjects refer to the very same thing or person. Here are some more doubling examples:

> <u>My teacher</u> *he* read us a story.
>
> <u>My friend and I</u> *we* ride the bus.
>
> <u>My sister</u> *she* loves football.

You need to pick one or the other:

> <u>My teacher</u> read us a story *or* <u>He</u> read us a story.
>
> <u>My friend and I</u> ride the bus *or* <u>We</u> ride the bus.
>
> <u>My sister</u> loves football *or* <u>She</u> loves football.

Teaching the Lesson (General Guidelines for Teachers)

1. Share the examples above, or make up your own examples to show how to change a double subject into a single subject.

2. Share the editing lesson on the following page. Students should read the passage aloud, looking and listening for double subjects and correcting them using the delete symbol and caret.

3. Ask them to edit individually first, then check with a partner.

4. When everyone is done, ask them to coach you as you edit the copy on an overhead transparency, correcting any errors you find.

5. When you finish, compare your revision to our suggestion on page 143.

Editing Goal: Correct 5 double sentence subjects.
Next, be on the lookout for *double subjects* in your own work.

Editing Practice

Double Subjects

The prairie is an amazing place. About 100 years ago,

the prairie it was mostly grassland. Bison and bear they once

roamed across this central part of our country. It is hard to

believe now. Farms they fill most of the prairie today. Some

scientists are working to bring back part of the prairie. These

scientists they are planting grasses and even bringing in

bison, elk, and butterflies to make the prairie more like it

used to be. The "new" prairie it will look more the way it did

when settlers headed west.

Edited Copy

Double Subjects
5 errors corrected

The prairie is an amazing place. About 100 years ago,

the prairie ~~it~~ was mostly grassland. Bison and bear ~~they~~ once

roamed across this central part of our country. It is hard to

believe now. Farms ~~they~~ fill most of the prairie today. Some

scientists are working to bring back part of the prairie. ~~These~~

~~scientists~~ They are planting grasses and even bringing in

bison, elk, and butterflies to make the prairie more like it

used to be. The "new" prairie ~~it~~ will look more the way it did

when settlers headed west.

Revising to Make Pictures

Trait Connection: **Word Choice**

Introduction

Have you ever seen a photo so out-of-focus you couldn't tell what you were looking at? Fuzzy writing is like that. Take the sentence *It went along the road. What* went along the road? What *kind* of road? We can bring this picture into focus by saying *The snapping turtle crept along the dirt road heading for the swamp.* Is that what you pictured at first? Or maybe you saw a semi truck cruising down the freeway— or a guy on a bike path, or . . . . The point is, you don't want readers picturing a truck when you are actually writing about a turtle. In this lesson, you'll get practice bringing writing "pictures" into focus.

Teacher's Sidebar . . .
The purpose of this lesson is not to encourage students to pack their writing with as many adjectives as possible. This only weighs the writing down. Encourage them to use precise nouns and vivid verbs that create pictures (snapshots or movies) in a reader's mind.

Focus and Intent

This lesson is intended to help students:

- Understand the value of descriptive writing.
- Distinguish between vague and clear images.
- Revise a vague piece to create a clear picture.

Teaching the Lesson

Step 1: Introducing the Concept of Imagery (Pictures)

Begin by sharing the two examples provided here. Then, with your students, brainstorm descriptive sentences that "make a picture" by bringing a vague, out-of-focus image to life.

Can't quite see it . . .	I can picture it!
The tree was big.	The ancient oak towered over the house.
The person was upset.	The toddler screeched and hurled his shoe at me.
The animal looked scared.	_____

144

The mall was crowded.   _____

The snake moved.   _____

The test of good imagery is whether you can see it in your mind—or *hear*, *smell*, and *feel* it! It is fine to use other senses, besides vision, to create clear pictures for the reader.

Step 2: Making the Reading-Writing Connection

Share the following sample, or any favorite passage that creates a picture in the reader's mind. As you read aloud, ask students to close their eyes and concentrate on the picture the words make in their minds. Ask them to describe it—or even sketch it. How different would this picture be if Kate DiCamillo had simply written ". . . and the next minute, Winn-Dixie was going after that mouse"? How important are the words "furry bullet" and "shooting across the building"?

Sample

One minute, everything was quiet and serious and the preacher was going on and on and on; and the next minute, Winn-Dixie looked like a furry bullet, shooting across the building, chasing that mouse.

(Kate DiCamillo, *Because of Winn-Dixie*. 2000. Cambridge, MA: Candlewick Press, page 36.)

Step 3: Involving Students as Evaluators

Ask students to review Samples A and B, specifically considering imagery: Which one creates a clear picture in the reader's mind? Have students work with a partner, highlighting words or phrases that bring the picture to life, and underlining anything that needs revision to make it less fuzzy. Encourage students to note possible revisions in the right margin.

Discussing Results

Most students should find Sample B significantly stronger. Discuss differences between A and B, asking students how they might revise A to bring the picture into focus. A possible alternative to Sample A is provided.

Step 4: Modeling Revision

- Share Sample C (*Whole Class Revision*) with students. Read it aloud.
- Talk about whether the word choice helps create a clear image. (Most students should say *no.*)
- Invite students to coach you through a class revision, underlining words or phrases that could be more clear. Brainstorm alternatives and write in your favorites.
- When you finish, read your revised passage aloud. Do the words make a picture in your mind? (Compare your revision with ours, if you wish.)

Step 5: Revising with Partners

Share Sample D (*Revising with Partners*). Ask students to follow the basic steps you modeled with Sample C. *Working with partners*, they should:

- Read the passage aloud.
- Underline words or phrases that are vague and need revision.
- Revise by inserting language that creates clear pictures.
- Read the result aloud to hear the difference.

Step 6: Sharing and Discussing Results

When students have finished, ask several pairs of students to share their revisions aloud. How different are the various images your students created? (Feel free to share our suggested revision as "one possibility," not "the answer.") Emphasize the value of creating *one or two strong images* versus adding 20 adjectives to a lifeless piece! There is such a thing as overkill.

Next Steps

- We think Sample B from this lesson is fairly strong. If your students feel they can improve the imagery, encourage them to revise it.

- Use ideas from previous lessons (stronger leads or conclusions, additional details, stronger voice) to make further revisions to any samples from this lesson.

- Encourage students to look for opportunities to create just one strong image in any rough draft (of their own work). Do this routinely as part of revision.

- A good test of whether an image is strong is whether you can actually make a sketch of it—however rough. Based on the literature you share aloud or that your students read to themselves, create a "picture album" of strong images. Consider creating art to go with some of them. Recommended texts for strong imagery:
  - *Because of Winn-Dixie* by Kate DiCamillo. 2000. Cambridge, MA: Candlewick Press.
  - *All the Colors of the Earth* by Sheila Hamanaka. 1999. New York: HarperTrophy.
  - *Amos and Boris* by William Steig. 1992. New York: Farrar, Straus & Girroux.
  - *Everybody Needs a Rock* by Byrd Baylor. 1985. New York: Aladdin.
  - *Verdi* by Janell Cannon. 1997. New York: Harcourt.

- *For students who need a challenge:* Invite students to work in teams to create illustrated stories—with two or even three illustrations per story. The stronger the description, the more vivid (and easier to create) those illustrations will be.

Sample A

I needed a book from the top shelf of
the library. The librarian was too short to
reach it so she had to use a ladder. She
climbed up. She had a hard time reaching
the book. It was big. We waited and watched
her take the book from the shelf.

Sample B

Roller skating is harder than it looks. The first time I tried it, my rented skates pinched my toes so tight my feet fell asleep. My ankles buckled, and my arms kept whirling around like pinwheels. My toes pointed in so my feet kept crashing into each other like little bumper cars. I was so busy watching my feet, I never saw that crack in the sidewalk sneaking up on me. It was only a half inch wide, but it might as well have been a canyon. One wheel caught, and I flew into a petunia bed, landing on my butt and crushing 50 petunias into limp salad.

Suggested Revision of Sample A

I needed a book from the top shelf

about ten feet up.

of the library. The librarian was

only five feet tall,

~~too short to reach it~~ so she had to use

inched up step by step in her slippery shoes.

a ladder. She ~~climbed up.~~ She ~~had a~~

had to stand on her tiptoes to reach the book.

~~hard time reaching the book.~~ It was

almost three inches thick!   (held our breath)

~~big.~~ We ~~waited~~ and watched her ~~take~~

grasp the book in her fingertips.

~~the book from the shelf.~~

Sample C: Whole Class Revision

Last time I went to the park, I saw a dog.

He was kind of interesting looking.

He was chasing a squirrel. The squirrel

ran this way and then he ran that way.

He went really fast, but the dog went

right after him. They came around a

fence and the squirrel ran up a tree.

The dog was frustrated.

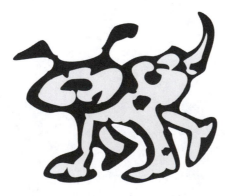

Sample D: Revising with Partners

Pilar ran across the muddy field. Rain fell on her. It was hard to run in the mud. The soccer ball was coming toward her. She could not see it too well. She kicked as hard as she could. The ball went into the net!

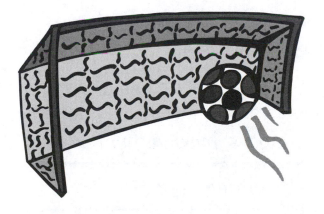

Suggested Revisions of C and D

Sample C: Whole Class Revision

Last time I went to the park, I saw a ^scruffy, gray dog.

He ~~was kind of interesting looking.~~ ^had a tail like a brush.

He was chasing a squirrel. The squirrel
^~~ran this way and then he ran that way.~~ zigzagged over the grass.

He ~~went really fast~~ ^zipped along, but the dog went

right after him. They came around a

fence and the squirrel ~~ran~~ ^scampered up a tree.

The dog ~~was frustrated.~~ ^ran around and around the tree, barking and panting.

Sample D: Revising with Partners

Pilar ran across the muddy field. Rain ~~fell~~ ^soaked her clothes and ran down her neck.

^~~on her. It was hard to run in the mud.~~ Thick mud caked her shoes, making them as heavy as stones. The

soccer ball was ~~coming toward~~ ^flying right at her. ~~She could~~

^~~not see it too well.~~ It was a white blur. She kicked as hard as she

could. The ball ~~went~~ ^(She felt her foot hit the ball.) sailed over the mud and right into the net!

End Punctuation: ?!.

Trait Connection: **Conventions**

Introduction (Share with students in our own words)

Writers in a hurry sometimes put the wrong punctuation mark at the end of a sentence—a period instead of a question mark, for example. Or, they forget to put in any punctuation. Then, their sentences might look like these:

> Why did she throw the ball to me.
> We ran as fast as we could, but we still missed the bus
> It's four o'clock

Reading your own writing aloud can help you catch little errors like this. If you read the first sentence aloud, do you hear a period? What do you hear? If you said question mark, you have a good editor's ear. What would you put at the end of sentence two? You might have said a period—or an exclamation point. How about sentence three? Most likely a period. The corrections would look like this:

> Why did she throw the ball to me?
> We ran as fast as we could, but we still missed the bus!
> It's four o'clock.

Teaching the Lesson (General Guidelines for Teachers)

1. Share the examples above, or make up your own examples to practice putting punctuation at the end of a sentence.
2. Share the editing lesson on the following page. Students should read the passage aloud, looking and listening for where sentences end, and punctuating them correctly. Remind them not to *overdo* the exclamation points—and to draw a circle around periods so they *show*.
3. Ask students to edit individually first, then check with a partner.
4. When everyone is done, ask them to coach you as you edit the copy on an overhead transparency, correcting any errors you find.
5. When you finish, read your edited copy aloud; then compare it with our suggested text on page 155.

Editing Goal: Fill in end punctuation for 8 sentences.
Then, be on the lookout for *missing or incorrect end punctuation* in your own work.

153

Editing Practice

Fill in End Punctuation

George Washington was the first president of the
United States He was born in 1732 and lived to be
67 years old Did you ever hear that Washington wore
a wig. Actually, he did not The truth is, he just
powdered his hair so it looked a little like a white wig
You might have heard that his teeth were made of
wood? In fact, they were made from the teeth of
other creatures, including elk Imagine that

Edited Copy

End Punctuation
8 sentences

George Washington was the first president of the

United States⊙He was born in 1732 and lived to be

67 years old⊙Did you ever hear that Washington wore

a wig⁇Actually, he did not⊙The truth is, he just

powdered his hair so it looked a little like a white wig⊙

You might have heard that his teeth were made of

wood⊙In fact, they were made from the teeth of

other creatures, including elk⊙Imagine that⟨!⟩

Revising for Action

Trait Connection: **Word Choice**

Introduction

Action verbs like *grab, fly, swirl, bellow,* or *sail* put energy into writing by making things move. Instead of a still photo, we have a video. A verb like *look* is what you might call a "quiet verb." We get the general idea—but it doesn't give the reader as much information as a livelier verb like *stare* or *squint*. Those verbs tell us not only that someone is *looking*—but also how they're doing it. In this lesson, you will revise by choosing verbs that show action.

Teacher's Sidebar . . .

Choosing one or two *just right verbs* is far more important than exchanging *every* verb for a more interesting substitute. Encourage students to identify two or three verbs in a revision sample that could benefit from some enlivening—and to revise just those. In our samples, we will offer many suggestions *for discussion purposes*, but we recommend keeping your own students' revisions light and manageable.

Focus and Intent

This lesson is intended to help students:

- Understand the importance of strong verbs.
- Distinguish between flat or quiet verbs and lively, active verbs.
- Revise a piece by replacing one, two, or more verbs.

Teaching the Lesson

Step 1: Introducing the Concept of lively Verbs

Begin by making sure every student knows what a *verb* is. Talk about "action" words, offer a few examples, and ask students to help you make a verb list. Next step: Talk about how a strong verb can give the reader just a little more information than a flatter, more quiet one: *John **raced** to home plate* tells much more than *John **went** to home plate*. With your students, brainstorm strong alternatives to the verbs in the left column. Always think about the meaning: What image are you trying to create? Two examples are given.

A little flat	**Lively and vivid**
1. Adelio **ate** his hot dog.	Adelio **wolfed down** his hot dog.
2. The cat **followed** the mouse.	The cat **stalked** the mouse.
3. Furiously, Adrian **put** the book on the table.	_____
4. Mom **moved** when she saw the alligator in the bathtub.	_____

Remember, don't choose any old verb *just because it's lively!* The *right* verb conveys just the meaning you want to fit the situation. Elephants don't "tiptoe" to the waterhole. Mice don't "thud" down the hallway. Also, feel free to use two or three words to get your meaning across: e.g., "wolfed down."

Step 2: Making the Reading-Writing Connection

Share the following sample, or any passage that shows creative use of strong verbs. As you read aloud, ask students to try acting out what they hear. Consider verbs the author *might* have chosen (other than *crept*, *dropping*, or *scuttled*). Did she make good choices? What if she had written, "I **came** out of the bushes and, **going** to all fours, **tiptoed** into the woods like a raccoon"? (**Note:** "Flags" are tall plants that grow in warm wetlands and swamps.)

Sample

I crept out of the flags and, dropping to all fours, scuttled into the woods like a raccoon.

(Jean Craighead George, *The Missing 'Gator of Gumbo Limbo*. 1992. New York: HarperCollins, page 34.)

Step 3: Involving Students as Evaluators

Ask students to review Samples A and B, specifically considering verbs: Which one has stronger verbs? Which has more energy? Have students work with a partner, highlighting verbs that work, and underlining any that should be replaced. Encourage them to note possible revisions in the right margin.

Discussing Results

Most students should find Sample B significantly stronger. Discuss differences between A and B, asking students how they might revise A to make it more lively. A possible alternative to Sample A is provided if you wish to share it. (Keep in mind that we have revised more verbs than your students need to take on. Good choices matter more than the number of revisions.)

Step 4: Modeling Revision

- Share Sample C (*Whole Class Revision*) with students. Read it aloud.

- Talk about whether the verbs in Sample C give the writing *energy*—and whether they are the best choices to convey meaning. (Most students will likely say *no.*) Invite students to coach you through a class revision, underlining verbs that could be livelier and revising them.

- When you finish, read your revised passage aloud. Do you hear a difference? (Compare your revision with ours, if you wish.)

Step 5: Revising with Partners

Share Sample D (*Revising with Partners*). Ask students to follow the basic steps you modeled with Sample C. *Working with partners,* they should:

- Read the passage aloud.

- Underline *two* or *three* verbs that call for revision.

- Revise by inserting new verbs or phrases that add life and make meaning clear.

- Read the result aloud to hear the improvement.

Step 6: Sharing and Discussing Results

When students have finished, ask several pairs of students to share their revisions aloud. Did they tend to focus on the same verbs? (Feel free to share our suggested revision, pointing out that students need not revise as many verbs as we did.) Emphasize the value of replacing *one or two verbs* with stronger options.

Next Steps

- Encourage students to revise their own rough drafts by revising just *one or two* verbs—but making those revisions special. Tiny revisions have great power.

- Look up several verbs in a thesaurus or book of synonyms. Talk about various synonyms and the slight differences for each one. For example, the word *walk* could become *amble, stroll, glide, stride,* or *inch.* How are these words different? What pictures does each make in your mind?

- Listen for lively verbs in the writing you share aloud, and keep a class list of favorites. Recommended:

  - *The Missing 'Gator of Gumbo Limbo* by Jean Craighead George. 1992. New York: HarperCollins.

  - *Crickwing* by Janell Cannon. 2005. New York: Voyager Books.

  - *The Great Fuzz Frenzy* by Janet Stevens. 2005. New York: Harcourt.

- *I, Crocodile* by Fred Marcellino. 2002. New York: HarperTrophy.
- *Tornado* by Stephen Kramer. 1992. Minneapolis: CarolRhoda Books.

■ Provide writing opportunities that let students show off their verb power. Good topics include sports, travel (by car, bus, horseback, bicycle, skateboard, or on foot), pet or other animal stories, storm stories, or any other topic that involves motion. Think creatively: Cleaning a closet can be the subject of an action story!

■ *For students who need a challenge:* Create a "how-to" poem (How to be a roller skating champion, How to be a third grader, How to be a rock climber). Each poem should be 5 lines (or more) long, and each line should begin with a verb. For example,

How to Be a Roller Skating Champion

Glide gracefully . . .

Sail along trails and sidewalks—

Feel the wind in your hair,

Tear past non-moving objects . . .

Push yourself—

Love your wheels!

Sample A

The wildebeests began their long migration.

They moved across the great plains of Africa

in vast numbers. They made the dust rise.

When they got to the river, they went down

the bank and got in. They swam to the other

side and got out.

Sample B

Kira was playing center field for her softball team, the Eagles. Back and forth she danced, shifting her weight foot to foot, ready to move in any direction. As the batter stepped to the plate, Kira crouched down, bending her knees. Her eyes narrowed as she squinted at the ball. As the second the batter connected, Kira sprang to the right. She leaped high, snagging the ball, feeling it smack her mitt.

Suggested Revision of Sample A

The wildebeests began their long migration.

They ~~moved~~ across the great plains of Africa *pushed and shoved their way*

in vast numbers, ~~They made the dust rise.~~ *kicking up dust as they went.*

When they ~~got to~~ the river, they ~~went~~ down *approached* *slid*

the bank and ~~got~~ in. They ~~swam~~ to the other *splashed* *struggled*

side and ~~got~~ out. *scrambled*

Sample C: Whole Class Revision

À chimpanzee got angry at the zoo today. He picked up

a banana and tossed it at another chimp. Then he

pulled a shrub out of the ground and stepped on it!

He stuck out his tongue and made angry sounds at

the zookeeper!

Sample D: Revising with Partners

Su could not wait any longer to clean her closet. She moved to the door, afraid to open it. Finally, she pulled it open. Clothes came down on her head. Shoes came off the shelf. Toys fell onto the floor. Su moved back to get out of the way!

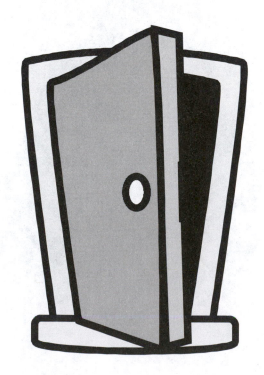

Suggested Revisions of C and D

Sample C: Whole Class Revision

A chimpanzee got angry at the zoo today. He ~~picked up~~ *grabbed*
a banana and ~~tossed~~ *hurled* it at another chimp. Then he
~~pulled~~ *yanked* a shrub out of the ground and ~~stepped~~ *stomped* on it!
He stuck out his tongue and ~~made angry sounds~~ *screeched* at

the zookeeper!

Suggested Revision of Sample D

Su could not wait any longer to clean her closet. She
~~moved~~ *crept* to the door, afraid to open it. Finally, she ~~pulled~~ *tugged*
it open. Clothes ~~came~~ *tumbled* down on her head. Shoes ~~came~~ *flew*
off the shelf. Toys ~~fell~~ *crashed* onto the floor. Su ~~moved~~ *jumped* back to

get out of the way!

16 Little Words

Trait Connection: **Conventions**

Introduction (Share with students in your own words)

Readers will sometimes excuse a writer for misspelling a word like *hippopotamus* or *antediluvian*. They are less forgiving about little words. Careful editors take extra time to make sure these (and other) small but important words are spelled right:

about	could	little	though	where
afraid	friend	should	thought	which
been	gone	their	through	while
before	have	there	when	would

Teaching the Lesson (General Guidelines for Teachers)

1. Share the examples above, asking students to write down the correct spelling before showing it to them. Ask which words give them the most trouble. Tell them which give *you* trouble! Are there others you and your students should add to this list? Keep it growing!

2. Make correct spellings of these words available and easily visible in BIG PRINT, either on a poster or in some other form. Keep them posted even after the lesson is over.

3. Share the editing lesson on the following page. Students should read the passage aloud, looking for misspelled words and correcting them. Encourage them to go through the copy more than once. Correct spellings are provided for them to use as they go.

4. Ask them to edit individually first, then check with a partner.

5. When everyone is done, ask them to coach you as you edit the same copy. To make corrections, cross out the misspelled word and write the correct version above it, using a caret.

6. When you finish, compare your edited copy with ours, page 168.

Editing Goal: Correct 11 misspelled words.
Then, be on the lookout for *little misspelled words* in your own work.

Editing Practice

Correct misspelled words.

about	could	little	though	where
afraid	friend	should	thought	which
been	gone	their	through	while
before	have	there	when	would

My freind Isabel and I where on our way to a friend's
house wen a huge dog came out from behind a
fence. He was growling, and both of us felt afraid.
We ran throo an opening in the fence, wich we
had not seen befor. There were steps on the other
side, and we dashed up ther. We wer out of breath
from running! I though to myself that we shoud
have gon a different way!

Edited Copy

16 Little Words
11 misspelled words corrected

My ~~freind~~ [friend] Isabel and I ~~where~~ [were] on our way to a friend's

house ~~wen~~ [when] a huge dog came out from behind a

fence. He was growling, and both of us felt afraid.

We ran ~~throo~~ [through] an opening in the fence, ~~wich~~ [which] we

had not seen ~~befor~~ [before]. There were steps on the other

side, and we dashed up ~~ther~~ [there]. We ~~wer~~ [were] out of breath

from running! I ~~though~~ [thought] to myself that we ~~shoud~~ [should]

have ~~gon~~ [gone] a different way!

Revising to Combine Sentences

Trait Connection: **Sentence Fluency**

Introduction

Smooth writing flows like music. You can make your writing smoother by combining two (or sometimes more) short sentences into one longer sentence. Sentence combining helps you say more in fewer words. It also gets rid of that chop-chop-choppy sound that happens when you have too many short sentences in a row. In this lesson, you will revise by combining choppy sentences. Then, you can read the result aloud to see how musical you've made it!

Teacher's Sidebar . . .
Short sentences are not a bad thing. An occasional short sentence gives writing punch. Sentence combining, however, helps students build flexibility in creating sentences of widely varying length and structure. This not only gives writing interest, but makes the *act* of writing easier.

Focus and Intent

This lesson is intended to help students:

- Understand the value of combining sentences.
- Identify opportunities for sentence combining.
- Practice combining two short sentences to make one longer, stronger sentence.

Teaching the Lesson

Step 1: Introducing Sentence Combining

Begin by giving students a little warm-up combining just two short sentences. Two examples are given. Ask students to combine the other three sentence pairs on their own. Discuss the results. Feel free to invent your own examples if you sense they need additional practice. As you practice, show students how to combine by crossing out unneeded words and using an arrow to connect what is left of each sentence.

Two short sentences	Combined into one
1. Adolfo was a cat. He was frisky.	Adolfo was a frisky cat.
2. Sofia felt tired. She felt hungry, too.	Sofia felt tired and hungry.

3. The bear ran. He ran into the woods. _____

4. Uncle Bob drove along the road.
   He drove carefully.   _____

Step 2: Making the Reading-Writing Connection

Sentence "break out" can be as effective as sentence combining in helping students understand how sentences are built. Share Sample #1, or any passage that illustrates smooth, fluent writing. Then, ask students to break it into three or four short, choppy sentences. Share Sample #2 so they can compare. Did they "break out" the same four sentences we wrote?

Sample 1: Smooth and fluent

Juan raced from the dugout, waving a flag, and shouting that our team had won the game!

Sample 2: Choppy version

Juan raced from the dugout. He was waving a flag. He was shouting that our team had won. We had won the game!

Step 3: Involving Students as Evaluators

Ask students to review Samples A and B, specifically considering fluency: Which one sounds smooth and fluent? Which one sounds choppy? Note that it is important to *read the samples aloud* to decide. Have students work with a partner, underlining any sentence pairs they think could be combined. Encourage them to cross out words, use arrows, or make notes to show how they would combine sentences. Ask them to look for *one or two* pairs of sentences to combine.

Discussing Results

Most students should find Sample A significantly stronger. Discuss differences between A and B, asking students how they might revise B to make it smoother. A possible alternative to Sample B is provided. (We combined three pairs of sentences. Your students do not need to combine all three.)

Step 4: Modeling Revision

■ Share Sample C (*Whole Class Revision*) with students. Read it aloud.

■ Talk about whether the writing sounds smooth or choppy. (Most students should say *choppy.*) Invite students to coach you through a class revision, underlining sentences that could be combined, and then crossing out words as necessary and showing how to join them. Note: It is not necessary to combine more than two sentences at a time, but you should feel free to do so.

■ When you finish, read your revised passage aloud. Do you hear a difference? (Compare your revision with ours, if you wish.)

Step 5: Revising with Partners

Share Sample D (*Revising with Partners*). Ask students to follow the basic steps you modeled with Sample C. *Working with partners,* they should:

- Read the passage aloud.
- Underline sentence pairs that could be combined.
- Combine sentences by crossing out unneeded words and using arrows to show how remaining words should be joined.
- Read the result aloud to hear the improvement.

Step 6: Sharing and Discussing Results

When students have finished, ask several pairs of students to share their revisions aloud. Did they tend to combine the same sentence pairs? (Feel free to share our suggested revision, pointing out that students need not combine as many sentence pairs as we did.) Emphasize the value of combining even one pair of choppy sentences to give a paragraph a fresh sound.

Next Steps

- Encourage students to revise their own rough drafts by occasionally combining just two choppy sentences. This small adjustment changes the sound of a whole paragraph.

- Occasionally, take a long sentence apart to show how it would look and sound if written in a choppy fashion. "Disconnecting" helps many students see how longer sentences are built.

- Listen for fluent sentences in the literature you share aloud. While you do not need to actually count words, do pay attention to whether a writer tends to write long or short sentences—or some of each. Don't forget to include poetry! Recommended:
  - *Dogteam* by Gary Paulsen. 1995. New York: Delacorte Press.
  - *I'm in Charge of Celebrations* by Byrd Baylor. 1995. New York: Aladdin.
  - *My Man Blue* by Nikki Grimes. 1999. New York: Dial Books for Young Readers.

- *For students who need a challenge:* Invite students to create sets of two or three choppy sentences to exchange with partners for sentence combining practice. As students become more adept, increase the number of choppy sentences to three, four—or more.

Sample A

Many places in the United States are hot,

including Florida, Nevada, and Hawaii. The

hottest spot of all is Death Valley, California,

which has had temperatures over 130°

Fahrenheit. It is hotter still in the Sahara

Desert of Africa, where a temperature of

136° F has been recorded. Now, *that's* hot!

Sample B

The Nile River is in Africa. It is the longest river in the world. The Amazon River is in South America. It is not as long as the Nile River. It is mightier, though. It carries more water than any other river in the world.

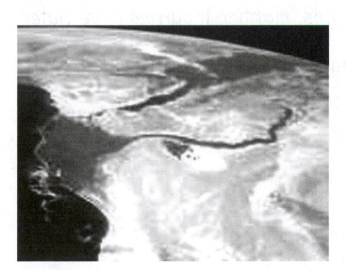

Suggested Revision of Sample B

The Nile River ~~is~~ in Africa. ~~It~~ is the longest

river in the world. The Amazon River ~~is~~ in

South America. ~~It~~ is not as long as the Nile
     but it
River, ~~It~~ is mightier. ~~though.~~ It carries more

water than any other river in the world.

Full revised text:

The Nile River in Africa is the longest

river in the world. The Amazon River in

South America is not as long as the Nile,

but it is mightier. It carries more water

than any other river in the world.

Sample C: Whole Class Revision

Dust is made of many things. Dust is made of earth. It is made of pet dander and human dander. Dust contains small bits of food. It contains small bits of plants. It contains salt from the ocean. No wonder we find dust everywhere!

Sample D: Revising with Partners

Javier was making soup. He felt happy. He knew

the soup would be good. He put some water in a pot.

He heated the water on the stove. He put in onions.

He also put in carrots. He also put in potatoes.

"This soup will be fantastic," he thought to himself.

Suggested Revisions of C and D

Sample C: Whole Class Revision

Dust is made of many things, ~~Dust is made of~~ *such as* earth, ~~It is made of~~ pet dander, and human dander. ~~Dust~~ *It* contains small bits of food, ~~It contains~~ small bits of plants, ~~It contains~~ *and* salt from the ocean. No wonder we find dust everywhere!

Sample D: Revising with Partners

Javier was making soup. He felt happy *because* he knew the soup would be good. He put some water in a pot *and* ~~He~~ *it* heated ~~the water~~ on the stove. He put in onions, ~~He also put in~~ carrots, *and* ~~He also put in~~ potatoes.

"This soup will be fantastic," he thought to himself.

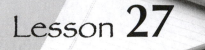

Putting It Together
(Lessons 21, 23, 25)

Trait Connection: **Conventions**

Introduction (Share with students in your own words)

In this lesson, you will have a chance to practice editing skills from Lessons 21, 23, and 25: getting rid of *double subjects*, filling in the right *end punctuation*, and making sure *16 little words* are all spelled correctly. Ready to put these all together? Here goes, then.

Teaching the Lesson (General Guidelines for Teachers)

1. Begin by reviewing strategies and rules applied in Lessons 21, 23, and 25: avoiding double subjects, including *correct* end punctuation, and spelling the "little words" correctly. Answer any questions students may have before proceeding.

2. Make sure students have access to the 16-word spelling list from Lesson 25.

3. Share the editing lesson on the following page. Students should read the passage aloud, looking *and listening* for things they wish to change. They will encounter three errors of each kind (nine errors in all).

4. Ask them to edit individually first, then check with a partner.

5. When everyone is done, ask them to coach you as you edit the same copy, making any changes you and they identify. Use carets and delete symbols to make your corrections.

6. When you finish, read your edited copy aloud to make sure you caught everything. If you wish, compare your version to ours, page 180.

Editing Goal: Correct 7 (or more) of 9 errors.
Next, look for editorial changes needed in your own work.

Editing Practice

- **Double subjects**
- **End punctuation**
- **Little words**

Mei Ling and I we were babysitting Mei Ling's little brother Jin, who is only two. We though he was taking a nap. As it turned out, he was wide awake. Who knew. Mei Ling and I we were watching a scary movie on TV. Weird music was playing and people were creeping through the shadows. Suddenly, their was a very loud noise. We jumped abowt ten feet straight up It was only Jin popping his birthday balloon. We screamed and then we laughed. Jin he laughed, too

Edited Copy

9 errors corrected

Mei Ling and I ~~we~~ were babysitting Mei Ling's little

brother Jin, who is only two. We *thought* ~~though~~ he was taking

a nap. As it turned out, he was wide awake. Who knew?

Mei Ling and I ~~we~~ were watching a scary movie on TV.

Weird music was playing and people were creeping

through the shadows. Suddenly, *there* ~~their~~ was a very loud

noise. We jumped *about* ~~abowt~~ ten feet straight up! It was only

Jin popping his birthday balloon. We screamed and then

we laughed. Jin ~~he~~ laughed, too.

Revising for Variety

Trait Connection: **Sentence Fluency**

Introduction

Writing flows smoothly when sentences begin in different ways. Not *every* sentence needs to begin differently, but some variety is a good thing. Fresh starts make writing interesting. Too much repetition can make your brain tired—and what happens then? Right. You stop paying attention. No one wants readers to drop out. In this lesson, you will revise to create sentence variety—and keep your readers tuned in.

Teacher's Sidebar . . .

Occasionally, repetition is used for emphasis—and this can be highly effective. A writer might say, *I can't dance. I don't dance. I won't dance.* This writer is repeating to sound emphatic. *I mean it and I won't change my mind*, is the message. This is very different from writing, *My cat is big. My cat is brown and white. My cat is a friendly cat.* This kind of writing can usually be improved with variety: *My cat Charley is big. He is mostly white with some brown spots. Wherever he goes, Charley makes friends.*

Focus and Intent

This lesson is intended to help students:

- Understand the value of variety.
- Identify opportunities to "say it differently."
- Practice revising for variety.

Teaching the Lesson

Step 1: Introducing the Concept of Variety

Begin by giving students a short practice in revising for variety. Write out the two examples. Read each passage aloud, asking students to identify the repeated words or phrases. Underline those. Together, brainstorm some "different ways to say it." As you practice, you may wish to explore different strategies: crossing out unneeded words, using new words, inserting pronouns (*he, she, they*, etc.), or combining sentences (see Lesson 26), to give sentences variety. (The first example is provided, but you may choose to revise differently.)

Repetitious

1. <u>Fred</u> was my friend. <u>Fred</u> lived next door to me. <u>Fred</u> and I played together a lot.

Revision

<u>My friend Fred</u> lived next door to me. <u>We</u> played together a lot.

Repetitious

2. Lions are big cats. Lions live in Africa. Lions hunt zebras and other animals for food.

Revision

_____

_____

Step 2: Making the Reading-Writing Connection

Share the following sample, or any passage that illustrates varied sentence beginnings. After reading it aloud, ask students to imagine how it might sound if the sentences all began the same way. (You might try revising this piece so that every sentence begins with the words "Each spring." What does this do to the fluency?)

Sample

Each spring there were new little spiders hatching out to take the place of the old. Most of them sailed away, on their balloons. But always two or three stayed and set up housekeeping in the doorway.

(*Charlotte's Web* by E. B. White. 1952, renewed 1980. New York: HarperCollins, page 183.)

Step 3: Involving Students as Evaluators

Ask students to review Samples A and B, specifically considering fluency: Which one sounds better? Which one has more variety? Note that it is important to read the samples aloud to decide. Have students work with a partner, underlining any sentence beginnings they feel need revision. Encourage them to use new words or pronouns, to combine sentences, or to rewrite sentences altogether, if they wish.

Discussing Results

Most students should find Sample A significantly stronger. Discuss differences between A and B, asking students how they might revise B to make it smoother. A possible alternative to Sample B is provided. (We have revised several sentences. Your students may revise just one—or more than one.)

Step 4: Modeling Revision

- Share Sample C (*Whole Class Revision*) with students. Read it aloud.
- Talk about whether the repetition works. (Most students will likely say *no.*) Invite students to coach you through a class revision, underlining

repetitive beginnings and rewriting sentences as necessary. Note: It is not essential to revise *every* sentence.

- When you finish, read your revision aloud. Do you hear a difference? (Compare your revision with ours, if you wish.)

Step 5: Revising with Partners

Share Sample D (*Revising with Partners*). Ask students to follow the basic steps you modeled with Sample C. *Working with partners,* they should:

- Read the passage aloud.
- Underline sentence beginnings that could be revised.
- Revise for variety by changing sentence beginnings, using pronouns, or combining or rewriting sentences.
- Read the result aloud to hear the improvement.

Step 6: Sharing and Discussing Results

When students have finished, ask several pairs of students to share their revisions aloud. Did they tend to revise the same sentences? (Feel free to share our suggested revision, pointing out that students need not rewrite every sentence beginning.) Emphasize the importance of using repetition only on purpose and for effect. It works occasionally—but not as a habit!

Next Steps

- Make a list of the many strategies a writer can use to put variety into sentences: e.g., rearranging words, using pronouns, combining sentences, writing the sentence a totally different way.

- Encourage students to read their own writing aloud, listening for repetition and revising—unless the repetition is done for effect.

- Listen for sentence variety in the literature you share aloud. Recommended:
  - *Charlotte's Web* by E. B. White. 1952, renewed 1980. New York: HarperCollins.
  - *Bill Nye the Science Guy's Big Blue Ocean* by Bill Nye. 2003. New York: Hyperion.
  - *Dr. DeSoto* by William Steig. 1982. New York: Farrar, Straus & Giroux.
  - *Sleeping Ugly* by Jane Yolen. 1997. New York: Putnam.
  - *The Table Where the Rich People Sit* by Byrd Baylor. 1998. New York: Aladdin.

- *For students who need a challenge:* Practice writing three sentences in which repetition is done deliberately and for effect. Doing it on purpose helps students hear the difference.

Sample A

My sister is my best friend. When I need someone to stick up for me, she does! If I can't think of something fun to do, my sister comes up with an idea. We have a good time together—<u>most</u> of the time! Even though she can be a pest, I still love her!

Sample B

Humpback whales migrate every year from Alaska to Hawaii and back. The humpbacks eat during the summer when they are in Alaska. Humpbacks eat almost nothing during the winter when they are in Hawaii. Humpback whales are about 15 feet long when they are born. But humpbacks grow to 30 feet in their first year!

Suggested Revision of Sample B

Every year, humpback
~~Humpback~~ whales migrate ~~every year~~ from Alaska

They
to Hawaii and back. ~~The humpbacks~~ eat during

During the winter, in Hawaii, they
the summer when they are in Alaska. ~~Humpbacks~~ eat

almost nothing ~~during the winter when they are in Hawaii~~

Humpback whales are about 15 feet long when they are
but with all that eating, they
born, ~~But humpbacks~~ grow to 30 feet in their first year!

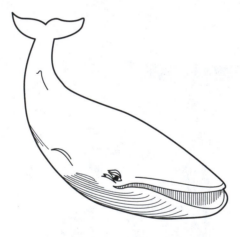

Note
Just moving words around a bit made all the difference in this example. It is helpful for writers to ask, "How else could I start this sentence?" The answer is usually right there in the sentence itself!

Sample C: Whole Class Revision

Buddy is my pet rat. Buddy is not a wild rat. He is known as a domestic rat. He is the kind of rat you get from a pet shop. He is very clean and neat. He is also tame. He would never bite anyone. Buddy is smart.

Sample D: Revising with Partners

Exercise is important. Exercise keeps you

healthy and fit. You can get exercise in many

ways. You can walk or run. You can go to the

gym. You can even stretch while you watch TV.

You need your exercise, so let's get moving!

Suggested Revisions of C and D

Sample C: Whole Class Revision

Buddy, ~~is~~ my pet rat, (is domestic, not) ~~Buddy is not a wild~~

~~rat. He is known as a domestic rat. He is~~ I got Buddy ~~the kind of rat you get~~ from a pet shop. ~~He~~ You might be surprised to find out that Buddy is very clean and neat. He is also tame, ~~He~~ and would never bite anyone. Best of all, Buddy is smart.

Sample D: Revising with Partners

(Walking, running, and going to the gym are just a few ways you) Exercise is important, because it ~~Exercise~~ keeps you healthy and fit. ~~You~~ can get exercise ~~in many~~

~~ways. You can walk or run. You can go to the~~ Also think about ~~gym. You can even~~ stretch~~ing~~ while you watch TV. Everyone ~~You~~ need~~s~~ ~~your~~ exercise, so let's get moving!

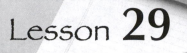

Editing Wrap~Up
(All Lessons)

Trait Connection: **Conventions**

Introduction (Share with students in your own words)

In this lesson, you will have a chance to put all your editing skills together in finding and correcting the kinds of errors and problems covered in *all* the previous editing lessons. An editing checklist is provided to remind you about what to look for. Take your time and read everything aloud. You may surprise yourself with how many editorial problems you will find—and fix!

Teaching the Lesson (General Guidelines for Teachers)

1. Share the editing checklist (page 191) and pass a copy of it out to students. Review anything that they do not recall.

2. Also make sure they have access to a written copy of the 16 little spelling words from Lesson 25.

3. Share the editing lesson on the following page. Students should read the passage aloud, looking *and listening* for errors or problems. They will encounter errors from various lessons, as well as overuse of exclamation points. They must use their good editor's judgment in deciding which exclamation points to keep or to cut!

4. Ask them to edit individually first, then check with a partner.

5. When everyone is done, ask them to coach you as you edit the same copy, making any changes you and they identify as needed. Use carets and delete symbols to make your corrections. *Tip:* Catch the errors first. Then, go back to cut exclamation points.

6. When you finish, read your edited copy aloud to make sure you caught everything. If you wish, compare your edited copy to ours, page 193.

**Editing Goal: Correct 7 (or more) of 10 errors;
reduce the number of exclamation points.
Next, look for editorial changes needed in your own work.**

Editing Checklist

___ I used carets (^) to insert words or corrections.

___ I used the delete symbol (⌀) to take things out.

___ Subjects and verbs match: ***They are***, not ***They is.***

___ I did NOT use too many exclamation points!!!!!!!!!

___ I used **capital letters** on names and to begin sentences.

___ I wrote ***My friend and I***—not ***Me and my friend.***

___ I wrote ***would have, could have, should have*** (not *of*).

___ I wrote ***My friend*** OR ***She,*** not ***My friend she*** . . .

___ I put the right punctuation at the end of each sentence: **. ! ?**

___ I checked "little words" to make sure they were spelled right.

___ I read the copy **2 times,** aloud *and* silently.

___ I **looked** *and* **listened** for errors.

___ I **double checked** my work with an editing partner.

I am a good copy editor!

___ Absolutely (checked 11 or more out of 13)

___ Getting there (checked 7 or more out of 13)

___ I'm working on it!

Editing Practice

Correct all errors.
Cut down on exclamation points.

Frogs are are interesting creatures! Frogs they

are found everywhere except where it is very cold!

Most frogs live in rain forests! They lay thousands

of eggs because some are eaten, so without lots of

eggs their would not be many frogs! Frogs start

life as tadpoles. Tadpoles don't legs. They do have

long tails, however. Later they grows hind legs and

then tiny front legs. When they grow into adults, they

live on land. Frogs they still like to be near water,

though. a frog's life is rather dangerous! They can be

eaten by snakes, birds, coyotes—and even humans! Me

and my friend brad once caught a bullfrog! We could

of eaten it, but we felt sorry for it and let it go

Edited Copy

(10 errors)

Frogs are ~~are~~ interesting creatures⊙ Frogs ~~they~~

are found everywhere except where it is very cold⊙

Most frogs live in rain forests⊙ They lay thousands

of eggs because some are eaten, so without lots of
                    there
eggs ~~their~~ would not be many frogs! Frogs start
                              have
life as tadpoles. Tadpoles don't legs. They do have

long tails, however. Later they grows hind legs and

then tiny front legs. When they grow into adults, they

live on land. Frogs ~~they~~ still like to be near water,

though. A frog's life is rather dangerous⊙ They can be

eaten by snakes, birds, coyotes—and even humans! ~~Me~~
                    and I
~~and~~ My friend Brad once caught a bullfrog⊙ We could
have
~~of~~ eaten it, but we felt sorry for it and let it go⊙

Note

We replaced 5 exclamation points with periods and added one missing period at the end (the eleventh error). The periods are circled to make them stand out. Your total may be different because this is a judgment call, not an error.

Revising to Cut Wordiness

Trait Connection: **Sentence Fluency**

Introduction

One of the best—and simplest—ways to revise writing is to cut words that are not needed. It isn't necessary to write, *She was short. In other words, she was not too tall.* The first sentence is enough. In this lesson, you will revise several pieces to cut words that only weigh sentences down.

Teacher's Sidebar . . .

Good writing isn't about counting words; it's about making every word count. For example, suppose a writer says, "A snarly black dog dashed around the corner, upsetting a flower cart." We could shorten this sentence by writing, "A dog dashed around the corner." But now we have lost *all the detail.* In this lesson, focus on cutting *what is not needed* without sacrificing meaning. In our examples, we may trim a bit more than your students will. Our purpose is only to illustrate *possibilities.*

Focus and Intent

This lesson is intended to help students:

- Understand the value of writing concisely.
- Identify opportunities to trim wordy phrases.
- Practice revising to cut wordiness.

Teaching the Lesson

Step 1: Introducing the Concept of Wordiness

Begin by giving students practice in trimming wordy expressions. Read each practice passage aloud and ask students to identify words that could be cut *without altering meaning.* Cross those out and read the result. If you need to add a word or two to smooth the phrasing, use carets (^). Feel free to move words around or make any other revisions. One example is provided.

1. Cats are good hunters. Because they are such good hunters, they can find mice no matter where those creatures hide.

Revision

~~Cats are good hunters.~~ Because ~~they~~ are such good hunters,
cats
they can find mice no matter where those creatures hide.

2. It was cold outside so I put on a warm coat because it was very chilly.

3. Bill went outside. That's where the mailbox was. He walked to the mailbox at the end of the road to pick up the mail.

Step 2: Making the Reading-Writing Connection

Author Seymour Simon is a master at saying things in a concise way—and making words count. Notice how much information he packs into the following short passage. Would you cut anything? If you did, would you lose important information?

Sample

Make a fist. This is about the size of your heart. Sixty to one hundred times every minute your heart muscles squeeze together and push blood round your body through tubes called blood vessels.

(From *The Heart: Our Circulatory System* by Seymour Simon. 1996. New York: HarperCollins. Page 4.)

Step 3: Involving Students as Evaluators

Ask students to review Samples A and B, specifically considering fluency: Which one is more concise? Have students work with a partner, crossing out any words that could be cut, and inserting any words needed for revision.

Discussing Results

Most students should find Sample B stronger. Discuss differences between A and B, asking students what they might cut from A. One possible revision of Sample A is provided.

Step 4: Modeling Revision

- Share Sample C (*Whole Class Revision*) with students. Read it aloud.
- Talk about whether it is wordy. (Most students should say *yes.*) Invite students to coach you through a class revision, crossing out what is not needed.
- When you finish, read your revised passage aloud. Do you hear a difference? (Compare your revision with ours, if you wish.)

Step 5: Revising with Partners

Pass out copies of Sample D (*Revising with Partners*). Ask students to follow the basic steps you modeled with Sample C. *Working with partners,* they should:

- Read the passage aloud—more than once, if that helps.
- Cut any words or phrases that are not needed.
- Use carets (^) to insert any words needed to smooth the flow.
- Read the result aloud to hear the difference.

Step 6: Sharing and Discussing Results

When students have finished, ask several pairs of students to share their revisions aloud. Who cut the most? (Feel free to share our suggested revision, keeping in mind that students need not cut as much as we did.) Remind students that revising to eliminate wordiness is like giving your writing a haircut. A trim is an improvement—but too much can ruin the effect!

Next Steps

- Encourage students to routinely read *their own writing* aloud, always looking for small words or phrases that could be trimmed.

- Pull a short passage from a textbook, e-mail, or advertisement and word process it in large print (16 point or more), triple spaced. Ask students to read it aloud, checking for words that could be cut. If you don't find any, give the passage a *Concise Writing Award*—and check out some other samples!

- Listen for concise—or not so concise—language in the writing you share with students aloud. Advertisements are often wordy and repetitive. For *concise* writing, check recipes, film or book summaries, or directions. Recommended books:
  - *The Heart: Our Circulatory System* by Seymour Simon. 2006. New York: HarperCollins.
  - *A Mother's Journey* by Sandra Markle. 2006. Watertown, MA: Charlesbridge.
  - *Whales* by Seymour Simon. 2006. New York: Collins.

- *For students who need a challenge:* Invite students to create wordy passages *on purpose*—then exchange them with partners for a "haircut"!

Sample A

Our neighbor Buzz trimmed the pine tree in his front yard. He trimmed it to make it look nice. He started trimming by trimming the lower branches on one side. But then the tree wasn't even! So he kept on going and he trimmed the branches on the other side. It was still uneven! He trimmed more and more, and by the time he got done trimming all the branches, there was hardly anything left!

Sample B

A few years ago, there were almost no wolves left alive in the U.S. Some people wanted to save these intelligent animals. They moved a small pack of them to Yellowstone Park. The wolves thrived! They hunted rabbits and small antelope. Over the years, that little pack of 30 wolves grew to almost 400. Today, many tourists go to Yellowstone just to see the wolves.

Suggested Revision of Sample A

Our neighbor Buzz trimmed the pine tree in his front

yard. ~~He trimmed it~~ to make it look nice. He started

~~trimming~~ by trimming the lower branches on one side.

But then the tree wasn't even! So he ~~kept on going and~~

~~he~~ trimmed the branches on the other side. It was still

uneven! ~~He trimmed more and more, and~~ By the time

he got done, ~~trimming all the branches,~~ there was

hardly anything left!

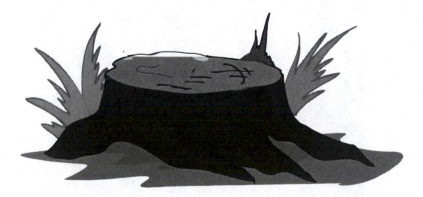

Sample C: Whole Class Revision

Basketball is one thing I am good at. I think it is my best sport. When I am close to the basket, I can usually make a lay-up shot. I am good at other things, too. I can dribble well and I can also pass really well, too. Once I did something amazing! I made a three-pointer! Basketball is definitely my best sport.

Sample D: Revising with Partners

Uncle Ernie loves to take pictures. He takes pictures at every party. Unfortunately, the problem is, he is not very good at it! In fact, he is terrible at it! One thing he does is that he moves the camera so that he never gets anybody's head in the picture. Later, when we look at the picture, we can't tell who we're looking at!

Suggested Revisions of C and D

Sample C: Whole Class Revision

Basketball is one thing I am good at. ~~I think it is my best sport. When I am close to the basket,~~ I can usually make a lay-up shot. ~~I am good at other things, too.~~ I can dribble well and ~~I can also~~ pass ~~really~~ well, too. Once I ~~did something amazing! I~~ made a three-pointer! Basketball is definitely my best sport.

Sample D: Revising with Partners

Uncle Ernie ~~loves to take pictures. He~~ takes pictures at every party. Unfortunately, ~~the problem is, he is not very good at it! In fact,~~ he is terrible at it! ~~One thing he does is that~~ He moves the camera so that he never gets anybody's head in the picture. Later, ~~when we look at the picture,~~ we can't tell who we're looking at!